LIVING AUTHENTICALLY

Living Authentically

... in a World that Would Rather You Didn't

BRADFORD L. GLASS

Special thanks to:
Stephen T. Glass
and
Janet L. Dwinells
whose love and support
made this book possible

To be nobody-but-yourself—in a world which is doing its best, night and day, to make you everybody else—means to fight the hardest battle which any human being can fight; and never stop fighting.

– e. e. cummings, (1958)

Living Authentically
... in a World That Would Rather You Didn't

Part I
Bridging Worlds Apart

Part II
Pathways to Your Unique Truth

Part III
Conclusion

Living Authentically

... in a World That Would Rather You Didn't

Part I

Bridging Worlds Apart

Introduction

The Pull of Two Worlds

"A bird sitting on a tree is never afraid of the branch breaking, because her trust is not on the branch, but on its own wings."

— Unknown

INTRODUCTION

The idea:

> **Living authentically:** your unique truth is *energy* deep within you; it's the quiet yet persistent pull of your deepest longing ... energy that wants to express itself through how you live your life. Its voice is so naturally *you* that you may have missed it altogether. The potential to live from this innate essence has always been inside you, yet may have become hidden underneath a host of lessons, assumptions and beliefs you've come to think of as the real you—but are not.

> **In a world that would rather you didn't:** society doesn't want you to think for yourself or stand out from the crowd. Taking personal responsibility represents a threat to a culture of social acceptance, consumerism and compliance. Your unconscious mind doesn't want you to think for yourself, either. That's a threat to old lessons and assumptions about how life, and you, are supposed to work, the validity of which the unconscious mind *believes* keep you free from danger. In fact, the more you *do* stand for your authentic truth, the *greater* the pressure you experience to stop.

This book is about learning how to place your *trust* consciously in **your own inner truth** rather than **un**consciously in the **external world**, a world, by the way, that is more *dissatisfied* and **un**trusting than ever. As the quote above suggests, how do you learn to trust your wings?

~~~

Trust consciously ... in your own deepest truth, rather than unconsciously ... in a clueless, distracted external world.

~~~

I've been there: lost, disillusioned, overwhelmed, afraid. I lived 30 years chasing a dream to nowhere. I believed it led everywhere. It didn't. I ate well, but was starving. My life has changed dramatically in the past 20 years, and the experience has proven to me that the potential for change like this lives inside each of us. In part, this is my story—how my life changed me. From a larger perspective, however, it's also an invitation—to unleash the limitless potential living inside *you*.

In having chosen this book, you've already demonstrated your willingness to develop. That matters. Here's why. In the pages ahead, you'll encounter some new ideas, and probably new slants on old ideas. You may have read, studied or tried many of them long before today. This book doesn't ask you to know anything ahead of time. As a matter of fact, "old knowing" can often be a deterrent to "new learning." I say this because one idea that might be new is that when confronted with anything (or anyone) that's "different," we have a tendency, albeit an unconscious one, to listen, not for learning, but by judging ... judging whether that someone, or something, fits what we already know. When we listen this way, even unconsciously, we listen for what we can find *wrong*. If you choose to listen that way here, you won't be disappointed; because you'll find something ... *wrong*. But if you're looking to find new *possibility*, listening "as a beginner," then *you* won't be disappointed, either; because you'll find plenty to learn ... *possibility*. An open mind allows new potential to rush in, even into spaces you may have thought were already full. So I invite you to consciously release judgment, perhaps even everything you know ... or at least catch yourself when that judgment inevitably creeps in. Because *how* you listen is a choice. Perhaps another new idea!

Hence this book, created with the intention of offering you *a path to your authentic self*. In its pages, you'll discover:

- the power of human *potential* (yes, including your own)—where it comes from, and what it means to live it

- the *obstacles* that commonly inhibit manifesting that potential (yes, including challenges you no doubt face)— where they come from, how you might release their grasp

- a path that leads to a place *beyond* the stress, dissatisfaction and anxiety that may characterize your world today—how you might actually *create* a bold, new framework for your life, then simply step onto that giant stage each day

- a set of *practices* that can help guide you to make your life your own, evoking the limitless potential inside you— ways to shift from "knowing" to the "*felt experience* of knowing," key to true change

- a set of practices that can help you *sustain* the changes you make, guiding you to regenerate yourself anew, each day—so the external world no longer traps you with its demands and opinions.

Why is this program different? Most programs in personal development seem to focus on one of two themes: 1) becoming more "spiritual," then just *allowing* growth to happen, "naturally," or 2) changing certain behaviors, thereby *forcing* growth to happen, "unnaturally." From my choice of language here, it's clear I'm not a fan of either. Why? The first appears to *take away* your personal power, releasing it to a "higher authority." The second appears to give you *unlimited* personal power, relegating you to brute-force your way through. The lure of both these approaches is that they offer short-term appeal. Aside from the fact that we've become obsessed with short-term results, solutions like these lead only to short-term results, too. Neither connects you with your authentic power. Authentic power is natural; it's inside you. It's also sustainable—for a lifetime. True, it may have atrophied over years of unconscious neglect, but it's there, waiting for you to reclaim it. The process to do that is one of *discovery*. Experience, both in my own life as well as working with clients, has left me with a strong conviction that "lasting change" is the result of gaining deep awareness, clarity and perspective on the ways of believing, seeing, thinking and speaking that underlie your everyday behavior and your connection with all of life. By reclaiming the power of your consciousness—which has always lived inside you—you never have to borrow or steal energy from others or the world again. *You* are your own sustainable ecosystem. And although this doesn't happen overnight, it is more effective, lasting and satisfying than any short-term result could ever be.

~~~

I realize that my message runs counter to much of today's "prevailing wisdom." Although I will show you why that is so, as well as how to maneuver beyond society's pressures, I also know from personal experience that it takes courage, openness and persistence to release the stranglehold of old beliefs and thinking. In fact, it takes courage, openness and persistence even to believe it's *possible to do so*. Such is the hidden power of "prevailing wisdom." The view from the other side, however, offers a sense of peace and freedom you probably can't imagine today. Over the past twenty years, I've guided hundreds of people in this work. This book emerged in part from those experiences. It's also a result of my own continuing journey. So if even the *idea* of this sounds attractive to you, come along for the ride. And if you're doubtful or skeptical, come along for the ride anyway; see if you can save judgment for later.

THE DILEMMA OF OUR LIVES

Here's an overview of what I see as the core dilemma of our lives—the pull of two worlds—a pull that is exacerbated by our general lack of awareness that it's happening, and by our tendency to get lost in life's everyday details (and problems) rather than the far more powerful energy driving life's big picture (and potential). Each of these worlds offers us a different "map" to the territory of our lives; each asks us to adopt *its* paths as our guide to living. In our heads-down relationship with life, we miss, consciously at least, this conflict, and are therefore unaware of the toll it takes on our being. Not coincidentally, we also miss the fact that, unconsciously, we're always choosing the map that takes us *away* from our dreams, not toward them.

The first map purports to depict the **external** world; its pull is direct, strong, tenacious, pervasive. Society has taught that in order to "make it" in this complex, chaotic, uncertain and therefore seemingly-hostile world, you have to know how to play the game. The rules of this game are continually reinforced over the course of your life—in messages from parents, teachers, managers, peers, society and media (the external world). The message: if you know more, try harder, stay busy, be productive, don't rock the boat, and get it all right ... you'll make a lot of money, be able to buy a lot of stuff, and in so doing, be happy. Does this sound familiar? We even have a name for this game: we call it the American Dream; and most of us have become quite expert at playing. It seems, however, that for all the *playing*, there's not much *winning* going on. Chapter 2, "The Landscape of Our Lives," explores this map in some detail, along with the obstacles it presents, obstacles that inhibit you from living your own innermost truth.

The second map depicts your **internal** world; its pull is subtle, personal, often indirect, yet persistent. Showing up in intuition, dreams, recurring life patterns, energy and sensations in your body, its message is this: inside you is a natural, creative essence, energy that makes you unique, energy that wants to express itself through how you live your life. You feel its pull many times a day, showing you your truth, asking you to listen. In fact, it *keeps* pulling at you until you *do* listen. It's the energy you feel when you are so involved in something you love that you're unaware of the passage of time. At its core is your *greatest potential*, your *authentic self.* Honoring your deepest truth transforms the way in which you experience life. There's a lot of *winning* to be had here, yet few are *playing.* Chapter 1, "The Power of Human Potential," opens you to this possibility, and the energy pulling you toward it.

It's compelling to go along with a game everyone else is playing. Yet to do so, you have to let go of *your own* game—your deepest truth, your biggest dreams. The problem is not that you chose this path consciously, but that because your unconscious chose for you, you don't have a clue it's happening. Biology "does this to us," by embedding repeated lessons in our unconscious minds so we don't have to think about them all the time. The evolutionary adaptive advantage here is significant. It would be tough if we had to consult a map to find our way home from work every day, or to read the users manual every time we wanted to brush our teeth. But evolution didn't count on some of the junk that would get poured into us as repeated lessons. Nonetheless, we've done as intended; we've *stopped thinking.* Even though we'd disagree with this thesis consciously, we prove its validity by responding habitually to almost everything. Old lessons now form a map of life, a map in which we believe so strongly that we don't question it. And it happens without our knowledge or consent, programmed under the illusion of protecting us from the unknown.

Because the clamoring, lure and perceived truth of external messages is so powerful, we often come to forget our inner messages. We live on unconscious auto-pilot. By living unconsciously, we deny the power of *our own voice*—favoring society's voice instead, and we deny the power of managing *our own thinking*, or life framework—favoring life's petty details and society's prevailing wisdom instead. So we can't possibly imagine that the stress we experience in life comes *not* from life, but from our trying to live a life that belongs to someone else.

Perhaps Mark Twain said it best: *"It ain't what you don't know that gets you into trouble. It's what you know for sure that just ain't so."* The rules of life's game are among the things we "know for sure." But one of the great dangers we face in our lives and society today is that many things we "know for sure" ... *"just ain't so."* The unquestioning acceptance of old adopted lessons has left us believing more strongly in what we *can't* do than in what we *can.* And as you'll discover in the pages ahead, *largely-unconscious* beliefs create your *largely-unconscious* thoughts, which define what you know of as *reality*. So while you may blame life, others, the world, and maybe even yourself, for the stress, lack of meaning, frustration, soullessness, and loss of spirit pervasive in your world today, evidence shows that *life* is not the culprit, but rather *how you believe, see and think about life* that holds you back. The implication is that if you're not living a life you love, it's because your unconscious belief system says you can't. It's time to get to know what's happening here.

~~~

The missing ingredient in living authentically is consciousness. *It's just as simple (and as difficult) as that.*

~~~

AN EXPERIMENT

As an experiential example of the theme of this book, I'd like you to recall two very different conversations. First, recall a difficult conversation you had with someone (or needed to have and didn't) in which you experienced feelings of stress, guilt, dread, anxiety, or fear. If you're like most, you don't have to go farther back than yesterday to find one of those. Recalling the conversation, take yourself back for a moment to the feelings you experienced then. Allow those feelings back inside you.

Now recall a conversation you've had with someone in which you experienced meaning, peace, flow, grace, ease and well-being. Take yourself back there for a moment; once again, allow the feelings back in.

We've all had both kinds of conversations. But did you ever stop to think about what makes your experiences so different? It's the same *you* in both conversations, right?

So here's where you might say, "Well, yeah, of course there's going to be a big difference; the circumstances were nowhere near alike." And here's where I might say, "Well, yeah, of course, but then again, *you* are not the same as your *circumstances*, are you?" Now what?

At this point we have a choice. As often happens in our real, everyday conversations, we could devolve into an **un**constructive conversation on why you're right and I'm wrong, or vice versa. *Or*, we could choose a more constructive path, consciously, and explore what's going on underneath the paradox. I intend to show *you* how to choose the second path everywhere you go in life, no matter: with whom, about what, the situation, the emotions involved or the stakes at hand.

And to capture the key point about the two conversations you recalled: it's meaningless who's right or wrong, simply because neither answer addresses the real problem. The key point is this: despite today's beliefs, the problem you have with conversations is never the conversation, nor is it the other person, the topic, the level of emotion, the stakes, your level of skill, or even whether you're an introvert or extravert. My claim is that the only thing making the two conversations you recalled different is that how you *see and think* about them is different.

Your way of thinking about a conversation changes the conversation. The underlying issue is that you don't realize the problem lies with your thinking, so you can't just go there to fix it. And that same habituated thinking tells you the solution lies in knowing more and trying harder. That would be great if you're stupid or lazy, but that is not the case, so knowing more and trying harder won't help. Yet as long as you *believe* this is true, you'll continue to miss the real opportunity. I want to go beyond that struggle, to a place of new possibility. I want to examine how you see and think—about yourself, others, life and world. That's a very different approach from one geared toward learning new skills.

By the way, I've had hundreds of thousands of conversations. So have you. I've hired people. I've fired people. I've had to plead my case. I've done performance reviews. I've disagreed with people about every conceivable topic—personal, professional, societal. I've been married. I've been divorced. I've brought up kids. I've helped bring up step-kids. And I have conversations with myself every day. Some have gone well; some have not. But the most significant thing to me is that, through these experiences, I've learned what makes a conversation constructive and what makes one fail. And because of those experiences, I've chosen to become a student of my life's "thinking environment" and now share that with others.

Communication is a metaphor for life. The phenomenon affecting your conversations is the same one affecting your life. You are a *natural* communicator; you always have been. You have an authentic self inside you; it's always been in there. Stop here for a moment; notice your reaction to these statements. Did you say to yourself, "yeah, but that's not true for me"? If so, that idea is a **thought**, and it's an example of how the way you *think* about life changes who you *are* in life. By seeing this way, you give your power to the beliefs living in your unconscious mind, leaving them in charge of how you approach your life.

If you need proof that these abilities are innate, observe young children at play. They interact without judgment, speak freely and with confidence, repair misunderstandings quickly, and connect at a far deeper level than with words alone. It's all completely natural for them—*until they learn they can't!* Most of us, often starting quite early, have unconsciously learned to censor our natural selves, a price we unwittingly pay in order to gain the approval of others. We learn we have to be nice to other people, work hard, get it all right, avoid mistakes, and worry about what others think. We adopt a self that makes us feel safe in this conditional world.

As an adult, you're so habituated into this way of being that you think this censored self is who you really are. Understanding this is key to living authentically. There is a real *you* that lives *inside* all the unexamined assumptions, lessons and beliefs you have adopted as the false *you*; and by reclaiming your authentic self, your truth will re-emerge, without effort—naturally. You don't "make" yourself authentic, you reclaim and evoke the authentic self already in there.

THE POWER OF CONTEXT

The same thing that makes a conversation constructive makes a conversation unconstructive. The same thing that makes life authentic makes life inauthentic. That thing is called ***context***. Context has nothing to do with the situation or with your level of skill (the places your habitual thinking tells you to look for answers). Context is an invisible framework around your conversations, and your relationships, and your work, and your vacations, and your life, made up of *how you see and think* about them. Until you become aware of it, context is the residual product of old lessons, and the bad habits they generate, which masquerade as reality and block your natural ability.

You *learned* to see and think this way, yet it's now so unconscious you're not aware it happened. Rarely do we stop and ask ourselves *how* we're thinking; we just assume we are, and we assume that what we're thinking is therefore real and valid. The only way you might recognize these adopted ways of seeing and thinking is by the shadow they cast in your life, limiting what's possible for you by showing up as "voices in your head," playing back old lessons 24/7, telling you how you're *supposed* to see and think. Examples: "I can't have this difficult conversation, because if I get it wrong, I'll get fired." "I can't possibly speak my truth, because he might not like me." The problem with these voices is that you *listen* to them. Worse, you don't *know* you're listening to them. Worse still, you don't know they're wrong. Yet they continually keep you from being the authentic person you truly are. Going back to the conversations you recalled earlier, the voices in your head told you one of them was different from the other. And the voices based their distinction in fear, not in truth. That's because these voices think they're upholding their role of protecting you from danger; and they see anything new as dangerous.

This is one of several ideas I want to offer. These ideas have made a huge difference in my life. I've experienced them at work in my clients' lives. I promise they can work for you, allowing your authentic self to emerge. Although you may find the ideas different from what you've heard before, maybe even to the point that you want to reject them, I promise that these ideas have the potential to impact your entire life. (In the chapters ahead, you'll find that the voice doing the rejecting is just one of the many voices of your old unconscious lessons ... one you still listen to, unconsciously, of course. You only "think" it's true.) Just as freely, I promise that if you're content only to hear new ideas, not much will change for you, no matter how inspiring you find them, and that you'll probably go back to doing exactly the same thing you did yesterday. Change depends on your doing something with new ideas; and that something is *practice*. As with any sport, you can't achieve mastery if you don't get off the couch. The same is true here; if you want to evoke the natural "you" inside, you can't just go to a workshop or read a book, even this one. You need to try on some things. But the cool thing is that it's far easier to change the way you see and think than it is to change life's circumstances, including all those people and situations that continually make you angry.

Because of the power this unconscious thought framework holds over your life and its well-being, you'll find that very little of this book is about managing the details, or *content* of life. I'm not going to help you "get more done." The everyday details that fill your day are not the problem. The focus of this book is the *context* within which those details happen—the framework of how you've come to see and think. It turns out that this thinking framework—the way you approach your day (and life) is the key factor in determining how your day (and life) will go.

Not only is 90% of this book about context, 90% of your effectiveness in life is about context, too, even though today you may not see it that way. Further, I suspect that 90% of the breakdowns, failures and problems you have are about context, not content. I also claim that if you learn to devote your life energy to being aware of, and choosing, the *context* of your life, then the *content* of your life will flow with effectiveness, meaning, power and grace—all on its own, naturally. A big issue is that we generally have little awareness of, or experience with, managing *how* we think. So we tend to reject it as a path of promise.

This book is organized so as to help you make your story both visible and conscious ... both the unlimited potential your life holds (Chapter 1), and the obstacles you face to manifesting that potential (Chapter 2). From there, you need a pathway to living your authentic self, a truth that has always been inside you (Chapter 3 and beyond).

I've chosen to write this book as a "field guide." Not only does this evoke the connection I experience with the natural world, but, like a nature field guide, this book could become for you a "companion for the journey." Like a nature field guide, it's not meant to be read and forgotten. It is meant, rather, to be experienced, to be referred back to, perhaps over and over, as you gradually evoke new layers of your authentic self. Each time you revisit a given topic, or renew your commitment to its practices, you delve more deeply into your own personal truth, experiencing it first-hand in a way that creates the meaning you long for, and evokes the authenticity you may only dream about today.

~~~

"It ain't what you don't know that gets you into trouble.
It's what you know for sure that just ain't so."
– Mark Twain

~~~

An Invitation

As you interpret *my* story, you'll find that you create an opening in your life, one where *your* story emerges. When you consciously write your own story, with both passion and pride, you, too, will no doubt experience the meaning and joy that have become such gifts to me. Although you won't always encounter smooth trails either, you will discover that your deepest truth offers more meaning and joy than you could have ever imagined receiving from the external world. As the unique fire burning inside you begins to fuel your journey and light your way, you'll wonder, as do I, why you ever listened to the outrageous yammering of a discontented world for so damned long.

My intention is to evoke that potential, energy that may have become trapped inside you, possibly for years, by the pressures of outdated beliefs and a demanding, yet largely clueless world.

So join me in a conversation that has become my life—to continually expand my perspective on the possibility life holds, step each day into the empty space I've created, then help others do the same. If you have the openness to allow new ideas to change you, and the determination and courage to challenge *conventional* thinking as a way to discover *your own*, we can explore together. Your answers are inside you; I'll keep the torch lit to illuminate your path, so you can find your way to your deepest longing, even in the dark. Along this "road not taken," you'll no doubt find, as have I, that the growing sense of self-trust and freedom you experience will become, and be, life's truest companion.

While discoveries you'll make in your journey are uniquely your own, the framework for personal inquiry tends to follow common threads for everyone. By adopting the ideas and practices suggested here, you will:

- Become willing to let go of the past, including who you *believe* you are, in favor of who you *really* are, the potential you may *become*

- Come to *know* yourself deeply, truthfully. Only by finding what is genuinely your own (instead of someone else's) can you truly *live* it

- Come to *trust* life, yourself, and your inner truth. Answers to the mysteries of an authentic, meaningful life are found only inside you

- Discover your *truth*, what matters so much that you want to design your life around its fulfillment (essence, uniqueness, passion, soul)
- Accept that life's *context* changes throughout life because *you* do. Living is a *process of continual inquiry, reflection and change*
- Choose *personal authenticity* over social acceptance
- Define and declare a *life context*, a huge "framework of possibility" for your life that embodies your intention, thinking and true self
- Be a *contribution*: bring your truth and gifts to a *community* of your choice
- Experience life's inevitable challenges and obstacles as *teachers*
- *Create "sacred work"* through the expression of your unique essence. If that work exists as a "job," go for it; if it doesn't, create it
- Experience nature as a connection to your deepest self, your source (this doesn't mean you'll end up hugging trees)
- *Be and do your best* in each moment. This means *remembering* your truth and intention, in each moment
- Listen to the natural *feedback* life offers; make continual corrections—to intention, thoughts, truth, words, actions—based not on a fixed agenda, but on how life's experience touches you each moment
- Treat yourself, others and life with *reverence* and *respect*

~~~

Your life becomes authentic when you become authentic.

~~~

Let's set out for the territory.

Chapter 1

The Power of Human Potential

"I went to the woods because I wished to live deliberately, to front only the essential facts of life, and to see if I could not learn what it had to teach, and not, when I came to die, discover that I had not lived."

–Henry David Thoreau, <u>*Walden*</u>

Introduction

I want to start by introducing your mind to new possibility—imagining a thriving future. Here, the word "imagine" means "envision without judgment" ... pretend, or experiment, even if only for a moment.

> *Imagine* for a moment that instead of the daily grind, you're living the life of your dreams, every day ... being wildly *creative and productive*, bringing your unique gifts to the world, year after year, with resilience, balance and meaning, regardless of life's circumstances. You can.

> *Imagine* for a moment that instead of feeling stressed or threatened with so much of life, you have such clarity and perspective—about yourself, others, life, work and the world—that you feel *confident and at ease* about your conversations, personal presence and impact, regardless of circumstances. You can.

> *Imagine* for a moment that instead of seeing life's chaos and challenges as threats to your well-being or self-image, you see them as invitations to your creative genius, and that you handle every one of them, personally and professionally, with *reverence and grace*, regardless of circumstances. You can.

To me, this is what it means to live authentically—deeply connected to yourself *and* the world; sourcing the energy for your days from deep inside you rather than from the outside; fully expressing your truth; experiencing the peace, freedom and joy that come from enriching your *inner* world while being a contribution to your *outer* world. This life eludes most, however, pressured as we feel by what we see as "reality"—life's challenge, chaos, uncertainty, stress and complexity. The only reality we know, we have more reason to *fight* it than to *question* it. A clue: did you find yourself greeting this imaginative exercise with curiosity and wonder, or by labeling it as useless?

Despite having glimpses into our most unique essence and truth *every* day, we often fall far short of experiencing it, on *any* day. That same experience has also taught me that this can change, often in an instant. It simply takes a new way of seeing.

Here's a story from my own past that changed my world in a morning and has continued to offer me possibility I'd never dreamed possible beforehand. It's an example of how a shift in ways of seeing can change your life ... often in an instant.

A MORNING WITH MONKS

Back in the 1980s, I was a manager in Digital Equipment Corporation's software business. After 10 years in engineering, I was "invited" to take responsibility for their software publishing and distribution business. I reminded the three vice presidents who interviewed me that I knew nothing about software publishing, manufacturing, or day-to-day operations. They told me *knowing nothing* was a job requirement. Perhaps I should have been more concerned by their response, but as a young, hard-driving perfectionist, I was convinced I could turn that business around. Besides, the work environment at DEC back then was one that allowed, even encouraged, exploration into frontiers of the possible.

Although I quickly discovered how scary a world I'd inherited, the fact that I couldn't admit my shortcomings made for even rockier going. But with this team came something new—an Organizational Development Manager. Although he was there only to help me, Jim struck me as rather strange. He talked about consciousness, awareness and being, ideas that made little sense to me back then. Like me, he knew nothing about operations; unlike me, he knew nothing about software, either ... more philosopher than computer guy. I was a problem for Jim; I didn't listen. One day, at a time when I couldn't imagine more than a half *hour* with him, he asked me to set aside a half *day*. I went nuts. The date being three months out, I had time to cancel.

I forgot. He found me the day before: "Meet me at 4:30am; we'll be back by noon." Screwed.

The sky began to lighten over beautiful country roads of central Massachusetts. Jim refused to say where we were going. My anxiety turned to fear, however, when we stopped at the top of a hill ... at St. Joseph's Abbey, a Trappist monastery in Spencer. (You may know them for their jams and jellies; and now, ales.) Father Robert was there waiting for us. Apparently, he and Jim were old friends. In silence, we watched a breathtaking sunrise. This moment of reverence and simple communion with nature would soon lead to reverence of a whole different sort.

The place scared me. With little religious upbringing, no exposure to monastic life, obsessed with getting things right, 30 miles from anywhere, and with no car keys, I had to swallow my profound discomfort. But, and perhaps in a futile attempt at self-distraction, I noticed an idea running through my head—a "model of life," a line, with pure **being** at one end (where I figured monks hung out), and pure **doing** at the other (where I was coming to understand I hung out). I finally caught on to why I was there, and it was probably a good thing Jim hadn't told me before the day began.

After the monks finished their morning rituals, a few of them joined us for breakfast. As uncomfortable as I felt being there, and for as little as I knew of their choice to live a contemplative life unhindered by the trappings of civilization, I was astounded by their conversation about topics that *were* totally comfortable to me—quantum science and the ways of the universe. As they spoke to their life journeys, I realized my view of the world had been quite small.

Father Robert began to talk about consciousness, awareness and being. (Uh-oh.) Then, in what seemed like pure coincidence, he drew a line, *my* "being-doing" line, but ... he drew it curving back on itself to form a circle, offering this as its reward: "As physicists reach the edges of what they can explain by science, they're coming to us monks to learn about the nature of being, so they can delve more deeply into mysteries of the universe. And as monks reach the edges of what we can understand with awareness and prayer, we're going to physicists to learn about the nature of the universe, so we can delve more deeply into the mysteries of being."

I was hooked. A scientist by education, an engineer by trade, and a thinker by nature, I felt my world transform in an instant. On one hand, I was terrified to feel the foundation of my entire life crumbling below my feet (a self-imagined world in which "doing" was worthy of high honor). On the other hand, I was filled with curiosity and wonder about the potential this new world might have in store. As Father Robert might have said, "Here beginneth life's journey." And so it did.

Mine is but one example of how life can change, even in a morning, through a "simple" shift in perspective, a shift that makes far more possible than in the moment before. Whether it happens overnight or gradually, you evoke new possibility (which is always there) by discovering the ways of seeing and thinking that have blocked you from it. You can wait for that chance moment, (when Jim "invites" you to breakfast with the monks); or you can realize that change like this can be an everyday occurrence when you choose to be open to new ways of seeing. Had I been more open, Jim might have evoked the same effect without such a "big event." Thirty years later, I'm grateful for how life has conspired to help me learn, and for how that day in particular created a crack in my armor big enough that light could shine through. It's difficult to look back and see the kind of person I was then, and nearly impossible to figure out how I thought it served me to be that way. Jim rescued me from an edge I didn't know I was on.

With hindsight comes clarity, and with that clarity, I see now that in trying so hard to manage life's details did those details fail me, and perhaps worse, that I *caused* the failure. A principle of Gestalt theory suggests that you're at your greatest risk of failure when you blindly rely on strategies that worked in the past. In the growing awareness of my thinking, I confirmed for myself both the power of consciousness and the power of choosing its framework, or *context*, then allowing life's details to unfold freely into the open space created. It began to sink in that I could achieve far more, with far less "effort," and certainly less stress, if I could learn simply to *see* more. There must be something about empty space that allows energy to manifest on my behalf. I suspect it's all about my own consciousness.

~~~

You're at your greatest risk of failure when you blindly rely on strategies that worked in the past.

~~~

EVOLVED FOR CREATIVE GENIUS

Because of this experience, I've become intrigued with how human consciousness works—*for* us and *against* us. I read; I observe; listen; I learn. I'm neither psychologist nor neurologist, but I'm a good observer; I'm open to new learning. I've become fascinated by what I've found. Of course, if a morning with monks could shatter my old world *and* create a huge opening to a new one, I wanted to know how the power of our consciousness can pull us forward to live with limitless potential, yet at the same time, hold us back in ways we associate more with life's circumstances than with our own thinking.

Two amazing aspects of our humanness have poised us for living authentically:

The Power of Human Consciousness: Evolution has endowed us with consciousness *unique* among earth's beings, one with the capacity to *imagine life into being.* We're well aware of the "everyday capacities" we have—to plan, to act, to make, to solve, to live, to complain, even to dream. But to *dream into being*! *That* may strike you as impossible, yet it's exactly the gift human evolution has conferred. It's almost as if it's our "destiny" to become the uniqueness inside; certainly, we have the consciousness to do so. Yet, the same power of awareness that allows us to *create* our own course in life also allows us to *deny* it—which it seems we do, by listening to messages *other* than those that make us the unique beings we are.

The Nature of Human Potential: Inside each of us lives a unique truth (essence, soul purpose, reason for being here). However you choose to think of it, it's energy that makes you *different* from everyone else. True, some of what's inside you makes you the *same* as others; but it's living your *uniqueness* that brings *meaning* to your life. Your authenticity is the home to personal freedom and self-trust. Think of it as a "seed" inside you that *knows its own path*. This energetic essence is *intended* to *learn*, *grow* and *express* itself in its own unique way throughout your life. The natural world offers a perfect metaphor here. Each of nature's creations has *its* own essence, too. Seeds possess the "knowledge" to become trees; caterpillars have the complete "program" to become butterflies. None, however, can, as can we, change the program as a way to redefine life's course.

~~~

"A seed hidden in the heart of an apple
is an orchard invisible."
– Welsh proverb

~~~

THE AUTHENTIC YOU

Authentic you lives *underneath* the everyday chatter you may know as "real life," underneath all the unexamined assumptions, lessons and beliefs you *believe* represent your own truth ... an adopted you. Your authentic self has amazing innate powers that draw you toward it, and toward your unique essence and potential:

- natural curiosity and wonder about life's (and your) mysteries,

- willingness to allow life's experiences to change you,

- tolerance for the unknown, uncertain, paradoxical,

- acceptance that "truth" depends on context and consciousness,

- deep personal longing ... energy that wants to express itself through how you live and work.

So, for a moment ... *imagine.* Imagine how life *could be.* Imagine the amazing dreams you once had all coming true. You know the dreams, the ones you might not even dare to dream anymore, because "real life" has gotten in the way, and "real life" doesn't look anything like you'd once imagined it. So you figured it was the dreams that were wrong, not life. Those dreams. *Listen* for the possibility your life represents.

Silently imagine yourself at the center of a universe of possibility. No matter which direction you turn, possibility is everywhere. Imagine that one of these possibilities touches you at a very deep level—the level of longing, yearning—drawing you toward it with its energy. So you take one step in that direction, now experiencing *yourself* at a deeper level. Then, from this new vantage point, one step in, you look around. Once again, you see possibilities everywhere, in all directions. Filled with the experience of the first step, you take another, again, in a direction to which you are inextricable drawn. You keep stepping in.

After days, weeks, or months of experience like this, all of it pulling you into inspired territory, you realize it's *just the way it is*, and maybe just the way it's going to be. Eventually, you feel yourself letting go ... of the need to plan, to predict, to know, to try, to worry. You're so immersed in each step that "where it leads" doesn't even cross your mind. You find yourself "at home," in way you'd never felt before. You might come to see this as *your* home, the home of the real *you*. You see others following different paths, yet all of them feeling just as fulfilled as you do. It's like they're all "at home," too. Interestingly, you also notice how wildly productive things are, results manifesting one after another, yet with no apparent effort, plans, agendas or goals ... not even any stress. How can this be?

Chances are good you identified, even if fleetingly, with the truth of your authentic self, the "you" you are here to be, that source of creative energy big enough to fuel a lifetime of "living authentically." Yet if this imaginative exercise instead seemed completely unrealistic to you, then you identified with "a world that would rather you didn't." Perhaps you experienced both—a paradox, a life of your dreams within such easy reach, yet the continual gnawing of all life's *shoulds*, constraints and stresses still all around you. More on these conflicting forces later.

One of the ways I've learned to reconcile such paradox in my own life is to stop, take a step back for a moment, and listen to how nature works. When I'm in nature, I experience life, its wonder and its mystery without the judgment and interpretation that often seem to cloud my endeavors in the everyday world. For me, nature has become a life-long companion, reliable guide to my inner truth, and compassionate listener to my toughest questions. In her silence, I've found answers to life's (and my own) greatest mysteries. Over the years, here's what I have learned from nature about living meaningfully and sustainably:

- The purpose of life isn't a result, but a *process*—of creative expression. The process of creating spawns amazing productivity with neither control nor agenda.

- Life is *opportunistic*, noticing possibilities generated by life's inherent uncertainty, then filling the voids with life. Without uncertainty, there'd be no opportunity, and then no need for creativity.

- Life listens to *feedback*, information inherent in every living system, allowing it to respond, easily and naturally in each moment, to conditions within the system. Life is a learning organism.

- With creativity, opportunity and feedback, nature creates order from chaos; *self-organization* is a *natural* process.

- In any moment, countless *simultaneous possibilities* always exist. By not choosing one ahead of time, even more potential manifests.

- Nature's *rhythms* and *cycles* ensure sustainability of life's process. Ebbs and flows assure resilience, balance, and renewal.

- *Cooperation* and *connectedness* create a thriving, creative, productive interdependent web of life. Everything exists "in relationship."

In this sense, perhaps nature's way is a perfect metaphor for the potential inside us, potential we are meant to live. Each of nature's elegant manifestations contains *its* own essence, too. A polar bear has in its DNA everything it needs to become the ultimate Arctic marine hunter. A maple seed contains all it has to "know" to become a beautiful maple tree, producing roots and leaves, sustaining the process to convert sunlight into energy to power its growth. But ... none of these creatures, best we know, has evolved, as have we, with *awareness* of its "knowing," so cannot choose to chart the course of life in any unique way. (A polar bear cannot, for example, claim it's tired of hunting seals, and decide to go to college so it can get a better job.)

~~~

You might begin to connect with the possibility your journey holds by entertaining a few *big questions* about life. Instead of being tempted to answer quickly, (such is our obsession with easy answers), see if you can instead just "live in the questions" a while. Living in the question begins to focus your attention and reflection and opens you to possibility you may have missed in the everyday race to live life. Besides, questions like these defy easy answers anyway, so choosing to be with them for a while opens you to deeper discovery.

- Is my life today a perfect reflection of my authentic truth?

- If I'm not living my own life today, whose life *am* I living?
- What's the story I tell about why I can't live my own truth?
- What would "my own life" even look like?
- What's the greatest potential my life represents?
- What would it mean for me to bring that potential to the world?
- What do I see as stopping me today from living my dreams?
- Am I willing to take bold new actions in order to get there?

We rarely ask such big questions, probably because they invite more self-reflection and patience than we've come to tolerate, and because we're afraid to turn our gaze inward, toward our hearts and souls. Each of us humans has the potential to create and live our biggest dream. Yet few do. Why? My experience says that the [only] missing ingredient here is *consciousness*—a level of consciousness that allows answers to these questions to become clear to the point of obviousness, where committed action involves no effort, no reminding, no excuses, no goals, and no dissonance with the external world. For most of us, that's not "everyday consciousness." Yet it is entirely possible.

Adopting this path takes courage and determination, not because it's difficult—which it isn't—but because today's consciousness, driven by your old mental map of life's territory, says that any new map must be wrong. As my first coach once put it, "trying to use *old* thinking to create *new* thinking is like trying to wash off paint with paint." Here's the key—because the map to your greatest potential is unique to *you*, you find it by looking inside you! You *discover* yourself. By getting to know how your thinking works *and* how it holds you back, to a level of clarity and depth uncommon in our world today, you learn to step beyond it, into the uncharted territory of your true potential. "What you *know* doesn't change you; the ***felt experience*** of what you know does. And *that* happens easily ... as a result of practicing it.

Here's what your deepest self has always known, (even if "you" don't):

- My essence, or truth, is already *inside* me .... always has been
- I get to know it by *discovering* it, via personal inquiry
- Life's path is created by *walking* it; it's not laid out ahead of time
- My *authentic truth* is a sustainable fuel supply to create my future
- *Uncertainty* and chaos are openings to creative opportunity
- Creativity and feedback *together* create *order*—naturally
- "*Truth*" isn't absolute; it depends on context
- *Meaning* comes from life's context and patterns, not its content
- All life is *connected*, existing in relationship with everything else
- Life is a *journey* (process), not a destination (result)
- Life is a *possibility* to live *into*, not an *expectation* to live *up to*
- I create possibility by how I *believe, see, think* and *speak*
- The *future* hasn't been invented, so it can be anything I create
- "*Impossible*" is only what's beyond my perception—today
- I'm responsible for the *framework* in which my life happens
- Life's natural *feedback* will guide my steps, in each moment
- Honoring feedback lets me truly *experience* my potential
- Living an extraordinary life comes from learning to *see* the extraordinary ... in each [ordinary] moment
- I stay on track with *practice*, consciously becoming the above

In retrospect, here's what I see now as having blocked me for so many years. The reason I (and I suspect others) don't know and live our truth is that we're missing both clarity and depth in three areas:

- We lack **intention**. We don't *have* what we want because we don't *know* what we want. Think of it as "intention deficit disorder." We're always committed to something, but rarely do we know consciously what that something is. In the absence of this knowing, what really motivates us is not getting things done, but what happens to us if we *don't*. That's fear, not intention.

- We lack **awareness**. Even if we knew what mattered, we're not aware enough to know what we're really doing *or* if it's getting us where we want to go. So we get sidetracked a lot. Example: We don't know what we really do with our time, yet blame time for our problems. Time is never the culprit; all we have is time. It's *energy* that's in limited supply, and we unconsciously choose to expend it on things that don't take us where we want to go.

- We lack **courage**. We *say* we're doing things to get ahead, but we're too busy making *someone else's* life work to take action needed to make *our own* work. We're giving away our life power. If *you* don't take charge of your life, society offers plenty who will … take charge of your life.

As one educated in the sciences, I've always had as suspicion that the framework of our own life's journey is mirrored in the journey the discipline of science has taken over the past few hundred years. Science is a "process," devised by humans, as a means to help explain the "truths" of the universe. Those truths are, and have always been. Coming to understand them, however, has involved the need for open minds, conscious awareness, curiosity and wonder, as well as a "discipline," or a process, to subject ideas to experiment. In this way, we've grown the body of our knowledge in amazing ways. It was considered "heresy" at his time when Copernicus "discovered" that the sun, not the earth, was at the center of the solar system. It always *was*, but we just didn't know, or believe, it. Fast forward 400 years, struggling to explain the nature of the very small, the *classical* ways of Copernicus, Newton and Descartes gave way to *quantum* science. Science reluctantly "gave up" on old ideas ... that "cause-and-effect" had to be obvious; that to be *true* means to be predictable, measurable and repeatable (it's not); and that matter is matter (not always). *Quantum* science sees an interconnected web of possibility, with time and space no longer constraints—a world of *energy*.

And it's the difficulty science has had in making this leap that I believe holds some of the dilemma, as well as promise, for how we see potential in our own lives. There are still "scientists" who fight off the "truth" of quantum physics. Just as there are plenty of us who fight off the idea that we cannot control our lives any more than science can now control an experiment.

Yet we're on the edge of yet another scientific revolution, one that sees *consciousness* as the driving force in the universe. In this subjective context, we *bring our world into being*, anew in each moment, through the powers of our intention, perspective and perception, *creating* life by walking the path. just Nature's wisdom has guided life in the universe since the dawn of creation, although we have only recently come to "know" it ... and even with that, the *ways* in which we know continue to change, often dramatically. As we begin to shift our thinking toward this new model, the potential our lives hold will multiply dramatically.

~~~

***Trying to use old thinking to create new thinking
is like trying to wash off paint with paint.***

~~~

An Invitation

Practice: take a few moments of quiet time each day. As a *rational* exercise, ponder the *idea* that your consciousness holds limitless power to create, that if your mind could be so clear and focused that nothing stood in its way, you could indeed manifest the life of your dreams. After gaining a level of comfort, then as an *imaginative* exercise, create in your mind a bold, vivid picture of you *actually living* this life. Because it's an exercise, there's no need to judge it, censor it or to think of ways it may *not* come true. Just imagine it *being* true. For now.

Future chapters (1) open you to the invisible web of consciousness, or *context*, (how you've learned to see and think) surrounding all of life's details, or *content*, and how, without your awareness, your context has blocked you from living your life potential; and (2) show how, by shifting your perspective from *trying to manage the content of your life* to instead becoming the observer, *designer and architect of its context,* you create a huge stage upon which the life of your potential can be played out.

Chapter 2

The Landscape of Our Lives

"The veil that clouds your eyes will be lifted by the hands that wove it."

– Kahlil Gibran, _The Prophet_

INTRODUCTION

The previous chapter, The Power of Human Potential, suggested life is intended to be a *conscious creation of the limitless possibility inside you—your authentic truth*. Both your truth *and* the capacity to manifest it are innately part of you. Yet if you're like most, *your* life may seem anything but that. So, despite what's pulling you toward your potential, there must also be obstacles that *keep* you from it.

This section explores the largely invisible forces that hold you back from living authentically. While it's the power of consciousness that can lead you to a life of joy and meaning, it's *also* the power of consciousness, in the form of **un**consciousness, that keeps you from that joy. The curious thing here is that it's not your level of skill, your level of effort, your willingness, other people, the world, or even life itself that holds you back, as you have more than likely been taught and come to believe. Instead, it's the invisible power your unconscious mind holds over you. Because you don't naturally "see" your mind at work, and because everything you've got stored in there tells you the problem lives outside you, you'd never "think" to look there.

This invisible "thought framework" that surrounds your life is both the fuel *and* steering mechanism for what you experience today as reality. You may believe "reality" has an independent existence in the outside world, yet it has none beyond what you give it with your thoughts, conscious or unconscious. Today's consciousness is more likely an *unconsciousness* instead. Life is living you rather than the other way around. Unaware that you're now trying to make your life work using the thinking of *others*, you can't imagine that your own consciousness is the culprit. Life *is* difficult. You *made* it that way ... but you don't "know" you did, so you don't believe it.

There are two major contributors to the "cloud of unconsciousness" that inhibit clarity of thought. One is called *personal context* and the other is *societal context*. Let's explore the hidden forces that deny you the life of your potential.

It turns out that as you come to know, consciously of course, where the cloud came from and what constitutes it, you regain power to release its fog that blocks your seeing and thinking. The amazing power of your innate consciousness is obviously key to creating the life you love; yet that same consciousness is also key to discovering the obstacles you've faced to doing that.

PERSONAL CONTEXT

Early in life, you learn "the way it is," lessons about how life (and you) are "supposed to be." Through repetition and reinforcement from parents, teachers, friends, managers, media and society, you came to believe these stories. Over time, with "practice," you turned them into a mental roadmap of life, a map made up of all you have experienced and learned, a map you come to believe validly depicts the territory in which you live. The edge of the map defines what you see as possible; anything beyond it is unknown, impossible. Evolution "helps" this process, the unconscious mind "programmed" to view *repetition*, not *validity*, as truth. Thusly programmed, you needn't think anymore. So you don't. And because all this happens without your conscious awareness or "choice," you *remain* unaware, either of its happening or its impact.

Think back to childhood lessons. They likely taught more about how life *should be* than about how life really *is*. You *should* be nice to others, you *should* do well in school, you *should* work hard, you *should* stay busy, you *should* worry about what others think, you *should* get a good job, you *should* make a lot of money, you *should* believe life is fair, you *should* control how life turns out, you *shouldn't* rock the boat. So, as a way to gain approval and acceptance from others (the external world), and as a way to feel safe in an uncertain world, you took these ideas as your own fixed beliefs. This led you eventually to see your entire world as both *outside* yourself *and conditional* (... if only ...).

By repeatedly following the same roads on this unconscious mental map, thinking becomes habitual. Essentially you *become* this map, unaware that you see life through this lens of the past. It's like driving with your hands on the rear-view mirror instead of the steering wheel. But you *think* you're looking ahead. In time, this map creates an invisible framework around you—a **personal context**. It's invisible because *how* you think is a part of yourself of which you're generally unaware.

Unlike roadmaps, however, your mental map describes a place that exists only in your head. You take the map everywhere; you know it as home; yet it was created by others; and it depicts no real place on earth. As long as you're content to keep doing the same thing each day, you have no reason to question any of this. If you want to learn anything new, however, you feel discomfort ... there's no road leading there. Unknown territory lies off your map, *outside the box*. If you continue to favor comfort over learning, habitually of course, you stay on the same roads. Following these well-worn paths leads you to believe more strongly in your *limitations* than in your *potential*. Life is an obstacle.

You might recognize these adopted ways of seeing and thinking, both personal and societal, by their road signs. There's the "be nice to others" road, the "I'm not good enough" road, the "I'm afraid of what others think of me" road. Challenges you face in the *present* trigger you onto one of these roads from the *past*, resulting in habitual response to life. The space not covered by roads is potential that is yours, but you're unable to access; worse, roads stop at the edge of your life experience, limiting you to what you already know.

Here are examples of old lessons, repeated sufficiently in our culture that they've commonly become adopted as "truths."

- there's "not enough" to go around (money, jobs, stuff, love), so I have to fight for my share

- *I'm* not good enough, so I must prove myself by knowing more, trying harder, and convincing others I am (good enough)
- mistakes lead to negative consequences, so I won't take any risks
- "truth" lies outside of me, in the external world; I must find it there
- what others say and think is a more reliable yardstick for my life than my own thoughts and feelings
- there's safety to be found by going along with the crowd
- there is one "right" truth, one "right" way, one "right" answer
- what happened in the past is a good predictor of the future
- I can't make a living doing what I love most
- Anything (or anyone) different—from me or from what I know—is scary, so should be avoided
- breaking things into smaller pieces allows me to control them ("simple" fragments are more important than "complex" wholeness)
- possessions, status, effort are measures of my integrity and success
- if staying busy leads to being productive, then being overwhelmed must be the key to having it all

As a brief exercise, consider each item on this list, asking yourself for each if you *believe* this value to be true (what your *mind* tells you.) Pause a few minutes after completing the list, then review it again, this time asking yourself if you *live as if* the value were true (what your *felt experience* tells you.) The differences between the two answers may surprise you. And that difference points to the unconscious nature of your beliefs, and how they impact your life ... without your awareness. Life may be an obstacle; but your *thinking* was its creator. Clue: every one of these "truths" is nothing more than a thought!

Societal Context

In addition to context at the personal level (telling you how *you* work), *society* impacts you, too. You're acculturated into a *collective context*, or "worldview," society's prevailing story about how *life and world* work. Worldviews change—slowly—over the course of generations. Here's a brief perspective:

> Our planet's original cultures lived in reverent and reciprocal relationship with **nature**. They listened to their world; in return, it taught them all they needed to know. Although their science predated modern *knowing*, they "knew without knowing," deeply and intuitively, that life was made of energy, consciousness, spirit—as one— ideas we are now "discovering" as if for the first time.

> Then, at some point in the still long-ago past, **religion** began to project a new worldview, one that dominated human cultures for hundreds of years ... and still does in many ways. Religion taught us to see soul and spirit as being *separate* from us instead of *part* of us, placing them "out there," where they could become objects of faith instead of subjects of personal truth. It gave our need for safety and certainty something to "believe in," but it *created* that something by taking it away from us.

> About 400 years ago, **science** began its reign as the prevailing lens through which we saw our world, explaining with *evidence* what previously lived in the domain of *faith*. But science recognizes only intellectual reason as a way of knowing, claiming life is linear, mechanistic, predictable, and repeatable—a world without inherent meaning. Human experience and consciousness fall outside this definition; yet they exist ... no matter *how* we know.

The aspect of worldview that matters here is that, as a society, we tend to adopt the "current best perspective" of how we understand *our world* as the perspective of how we understand *ourselves*, too. Although it may be obvious, there's a price we pay in making this correlation. In the case of religion, we lost connection with our own souls and spirits, which are, in fact, very much parts of us. In the case of science, we lost connection with our subjective humanness. There's nothing "wrong" with either religion or science. But to adopt one as a worldview gives it power to define a world it was never intended to define. Science is not the world; it is a *process* designed to help us *understand* certain aspects of our world. Big difference. Yet we're unaware of the disconnect.

Here are examples of societal messages, repeated sufficiently in our culture that they've commonly become adopted as "norms," without our personal inquiry, largely because we've been immersed in them so long they've become like the air we breathe.

Society tells us to value:

- social acceptance over personal authenticity
- answers over questions (better yet, right answers, and right now)
- compliance over creativity (be the same as others, not unique)
- busyness over silent reflection (busy means productive)
- expedience over completeness (get it done, now)
- drama over meaning (instant reactions vs. long-term cultivation)
- our limitations over our potential (we seem to love all we *can't* do)
- finding/fixing what's wrong over discovering what's possible
- external validation over inner truth ("they" can make/break a day)
- productivity over fulfillment
- scientific reason over subjective knowing

- science and technology as saviors for all our problems
- a rule ... that it's not OK to questions any of these rules

Now, as before, consider each item on this list, asking yourself for each if you *believe* this value to be true (what your *mind* tells you.) Pause a few minutes after completing the list, then review it again, this time asking yourself if you *live as if* the value were true (what your *felt experience* tells you.)

This entire collection of stories, both personal and societal—nothing more than a bunch of *thoughts*—has, with neither your awareness nor consent, created a cloud in front of you, obscuring your vision, filtering your thinking, and blocking your natural awareness and ability.

Because they describe only your external world, these thoughts have also robbed you of your *uniqueness* (the innate, creative essence that makes you **you**—or soul) and *oneness* (the connectedness we share with all life—or spirit—your true self).

~~~

The safety you truly desire in life lies in what you've traded away—your own inner truth.

~~~

LOST IN THE WILDERNESS

We're sure these stories are *truth* because they're all we ever learned; it requires little thought to simply go along with them. Plus, there's perceived safety in numbers if we do go along. We may even bristle if someone says we're on a dead-end street. *You* may even be bristling now—because I'm saying living this story takes you down a dead-end street. It's a dead-end street because it's *someone else's* street, not *your own*. If I were living someone else's life, I'd certainly feel lost. Yet that's where we are: lost in the wilderness using a map to somewhere else!

~~~

***You may react by saying, "Oh, no, none of this stuff
applies to me." To which I respond, "Yes, it does."***

~~~

What we experience as reality is the result of the thoughts
to which we give our energy, conscious or unconscious. The
problem with thinking being unconscious is that we have no
[conscious] power over it. So if we allow our thoughts to tell us
all the reasons we can't live our truth, we won't. If we choose
thoughts of self-trust and inner potential, we'll have *that* instead.
As long as a thought lives in the mind, and as long as you listen
to it, it will be true. And that's where the problem lies. If, by
contrast, you used your *conscious* mind to notice the workings of
your *unconscious* mind, first, you'd probably be quite surprised,
but certainly then become more open to new ideas.

How do you find your way home? How can you know where
and how you're being held hostage by old lessons and beliefs,
by the thinking of others? *Listen.* They speak. How? They show
up as "voices in your head." We all have voices in our heads. You
might not "hear" them as you would hear 25 people all talking
at the same time, but they make as much "noise." They're the
voices that tell you what to believe, think, say or do ... or *not*
believe, think, say or do. And *you* think you're thinking them.
They're probably screaming right now. You may have gotten so
used to them that you don't truly "hear" them, yet it's as if you'd
unknowingly rented your mind to a bunch of maniacs, and now
believe it's up to you to deal with them. Here's a sampling of
voices: I can't do that; she won't like me. This is impossible; I don't
dare to mess up, so I won't try. I'm not good enough for that. He's
always looking at me funny. Those voices. You know them, right?

There are a few problems with these voices.

- There's a big difference between something *being*
  impossible and a *thought* that it's impossible.

- The voices in your head are *thoughts*, not "reality."
- They were put there by *others*.
- They have no independent life of their own, because they live solely in your mind.
- The problem is not that the voices live there—in your head; we all have them.
- The problem is that you *listen* to them!!
- Another problem is that you don't know you're doing that.
- If you listen to them long enough (years, for most people) you even think these voices are *who you are*.
- You're not. And they're not. They're just #$%^&* *voices*!!

~~~

The problem we have with life is that we have misidentified the problem we have with life.

~~~

So the reason you don't live your truth, don't live your dreams, is that the voices in your head tell you that you can't. And you listen to them. Hard as it may be to believe, it's really no more than that.

We often have good "*stories*" about why we don't have what we want in life. (I will ... when I have the money, when my kids are out of school, when others think I'm OK, when *I* think I'm OK, when Mercury gets out of retrograde.) More voices. And they're nonsense. You'll have what you want when you *believe you can have it.* (another thought). By misidentifying the enemy as the *outer* world, you deny your own greatness, a permanent resident of your *inner* world (underneath all the voices, of course). The path to get there is to learn how to recognize these voices for what they truly are: *nonsense*. No thoughts have ever enjoyed *any* reality (or power over you) whatsoever beyond what you *give* them. So the "shift" here is to stop giving them your life. And, although it may seem counterintuitive, that happens by getting to know them in a non-judgmental, objective way. And you do *that* with the regular practice of personal self-reflection. What's left after that is the *real you.*

By the way, I have voices in my head, too: Hey, who do you think you are to do this work? I mean what do you have to offer? What makes you think you're better than they are? Aren't you afraid? Don't you know who you *really* are? What if they don't like you? What if they think you're a fraud? My writing, speaking and coaching are the result of a successful conversation—*with myself*—over and over, to *hear* voices but not *become* them. The voices are there. I am not my voices. It's a choice, one you can make only consciously ... and with practice.

This conflict always reminds me of a native American legend. An old Cherokee is teaching his grandson about life. "A fight is going on inside me," he said to the boy. "It is a terrible fight and it is between two wolves. One is evil—he is anger, envy, sorrow, regret, greed, arrogance, self-pity, guilt, resentment, inferiority, lies, false pride, superiority, and ego." He continued, "The other is good—he is joy, peace, love, hope, serenity, humility, kindness, benevolence, empathy, generosity, truth, compassion, and faith. The same fight is going on inside you—and inside every other person, too." The grandson thought about it for a minute and then asked his grandfather, "Which wolf will win?" The old Cherokee simply replied, "The one you feed."

Once you become consciously aware of these thoughts, you see them for the illusion they are. They're thoughts with little or no support in fact, merely echoes (albeit loud, persistent ones) from your ancient past. The problem is only that you *listen* to them. Worse, you don't *know* you listen to them. Worse still, you don't know they're untrue, or that they belong to others.

Curiously, you'll also see that few of the unconscious thoughts driving your life are about the *present*. The messages are made up of old lessons and experiences, unexamined assumptions, false beliefs, outdated views—all from the past. Some of the beliefs *take you back* to this past (with feelings like regret, guilt, resentment, anger). And some of the beliefs *take you to the future* (with feelings like anxiety, dread, worry). The Cherokee legend lives in each of us. Either way, they're simply old thoughts. Yet because you're largely unaware of them, (of their source or their impact), you've come to see them as defining who you really are. When you're lost in the past or the future, you're lost in *thoughts* about the past or future, not the *experience* of the past or future. Unaware, you miss entirely the experience of the present, which, by the way, is the only moment you *can* experience.

A Window into the Future

So here's a summary of where this process of learning, acculturation, habituation and unconscious living has left us (again, with some help from the Gestalt theory of human development):

- You tend to *use* what you're good at

- You *got* good at it either because it was innate in you *or* because you adopted it from old lessons (being responsible, victim, right, controlling, etc.), an unconscious response geared toward gaining approval from others

- When things get tough, you tend to *overuse* what you're good at—another unconscious response ... out of fear, need to control, or self-defense

- Over time, you *habituate* what you're good at; it becomes unconscious background, a comfort zone, a "prevailing strategy" you use *independent* of circumstances—even to a point of believing this is who you really are

- *Over-relying* on what you're good at limits your effectiveness, by blinding you to new choices and leaving you stuck or stressed from trying so hard

- Yet *none* of this is "truth." It's an artifact of the unconscious mind, voices in your head that run 24/7. The problem is that you *listen*!

- You're at your greatest risk of failure when you blindly continue to use what has worked in the past
- "The way things are" doesn't ask for your judgment or upset. It asks for your *acceptance* and *creative genius*
- The missing ingredient is neither skill nor effort, but *consciousness*
- You shift your consciousness through practice. *Awareness in this moment* is the most powerful tool you have for evoking change *in the next moment*

~~~

*"Let us spend one day as deliberately as Nature,
and not be thrown off track by every nutshell
and mosquito's wing that falls on the rails."
– Henry David Thoreau*

~~~

The voice of your *authentic self* continually, yet quietly, says, "I am; I trust; I know." To live authentically is to reclaim this true self, which you do by getting to know the voices of your *adopted self*, voices that block your truth. With this recognition comes the ability to make a *conscious* choice to *stop listening*. As you do, the voice of your personal truth emerges—naturally.

By contrast, your *adopted self* wants to protect you from danger; yet it has become acculturated to see anything new as danger. At the core of our belief system is the desire for *safety*. We've unknowingly turned this *natural* human need into an *unnatural* quest for *certainty* instead. Certainty such as this doesn't exist in a world uncertain by design. The safety we *truly* desire lies in what we've traded away—our own inner truth. Yet we unconsciously grow to *like* the adopted self, as well as the unconscious mind. The focus of that mind is keeping things the same, so we feel safe in their hands. There should be no surprise, then, why we create tomorrows that look alarmingly like yesterday.

So as we give precedence to the mind's incessant chatter over the reality in front of our faces, we might well conclude that

- we're *biologically* wired for curiosity and wonder, yet
- we're *culturally* wired to deny whatever we discover.

You change cultural wiring through a practice of growing awareness of the thoughts that created it.

It's not about learning new skills, but *un*-learning things that have blocked what's natural in you. You might see it as Michelangelo did with his statue of David. He said David was already "*in* the marble;" he had only to remove all that was "not David." Your path to living authentically is the same; the *only* thing you need to do is remove what's "not you"—a cloud of lessons, habits, experiences, beliefs and assumptions, adopted unconsciously, none of them examined or tested, probably for years, yet all of them conspiring to obscure your natural, authentic self. By purposefully *discovering* the ways of seeing and thinking that have *blocked* you from your potential, those blocks fall away, naturally, exposing and evoking your true nature underneath.

~~~

**Awareness in this moment is the most powerful tool
you have for evoking change in the next moment.**

~~~

This allows you to replace your old, outdated mental map with a new one, one that depicts the true territory of your life. That map is unique to you, simply because *you* are unique. So its paths are created by walking them, not by having them laid out ahead of time. You create it with one key ingredient—*awareness*—deep, clear, objective awareness of your consciousness. It's all a process of inner discovery. Creating an extraordinary future starts with knowing how your current ways of believing, seeing and thinking have systematically denied you of that future up until now. What you're discovering is not "your life story," but the "life story of your thinking." The next chapter, *The Path is Made by Walking It*, shows you how.

It's clear to me, and now, I trust, to you as well, that I have perhaps belabored the story about how your thinking became largely unconscious, and how forces outside of you have hijacked the forces inside you. This repetition and reinforced perspective is purposeful. My own life experience has shown me, and my experience with clients has reinforced this, that the power the unconscious mind has over us is such that nothing in our experience leaves us believing any of this could be so. Only the true felt experience of this dichotomy will help us shift. And (perhaps) only the purposeful repetition of its "story" will leave us open to gaining that experience. Read on.

Chapter 3

The Path is Made by Walking It

"Draw a different frame around the same set of circumstances and new pathways come into view. Find the right framework and extraordinary accomplishment becomes an everyday experience."

– Ben and Roz Zander, *The Art of Possibility*

INTRODUCTION

As the previous chapter showed, continual, often competing, pressures keep us from our dreams. Unaware they're caused by how we've come to think, we tend to blame *life* instead. By misidentifying the enemy, we either feel powerless to change, or try to solve the wrong problem.

Once you understand that these obstacles are part of your *unconsciously-chosen* life context, you can chart a new course, one that honors the authentic truth inside. The voices of life's "prevailing wisdom" never go away; you just stop listening. Besides, you now have *your own* voice to listen to, a voice that holds all the promise you need.

An analogy to show why awareness of these unconscious messages is so powerful: Imagine walking into a crowded room, perhaps one of those dreaded networking events, with 25 people talking at the same time. Although you won't be able to hear any of the conversations, you'll instantly be able to recognize the voice of a loved one, even blindfolded, in the middle of the din. The point is that you've developed a "pattern recognition system" for a familiar voice, one learned by repeatedly hearing it. If you think of the chatter in your unconscious mind as a collection of voices in your head, the practice of learning to recognize them works the same way. When you can identify each voice in the "crowded room" of your mind, you have a choice previously unavailable to you—to honor the voice (walk toward it) or reject it (walk away). Without such recognition, however, you have a problem: you **listen** to the voice, and unconsciously respond to its "truth."

I suggest that in order to develop pattern recognition skills that allow you to quell the voices limiting your authenticity and potential, you need to become practiced at listening *for* them (which is very different from listening *to* them), thereby learning to become aware of how they impact your life. A principle in Gestalt theory suggests that *deep, non-judgmental awareness and acceptance* of "the way it *is*" today is the most powerful tool you have to create "the way it *could be*" tomorrow. With that awareness alone, you expand perception, perspective and power of choice. The clarity gained opens big potential—access to your unique essence, home to your most authentic truth.

As your thinking changes, the edges of your world *expand* to include what now appears "impossible." The "impossible" things don't change; how you think about them does. As your consciousness expands, new possibility rushes in to fill the space created—the potential that is *you*.

FINDING OUR WAY HOME

Over 150 years ago, Henry David Thoreau "went to the woods"— so he could experience himself and his life from a perspective of personal clarity. Although he lived in a simpler time, to this day he stands as an icon of the human spirit, living simply and authentically, deeply connected with both his own truth and something far bigger than himself. From one perspective, he had very little. From another, his life was full of possibility; he had it all. Thoreau found and lived his truth; you can, too. You don't need to move to the woods (although it might help); yet you can live from your own inner essence, every single day.

Anywhere we look in history, we find other Thoreaus. John Muir, the Buddha, Jesus, Polynesian voyagers, and countless others ventured into nature as a way to find truth. Original cultures lived in reverence and reciprocity with nature. The harmony they experienced framed not only a rich way of life but a deep and authentic system of faith. To this day, native-style vision quests offer personal time in nature as a way to reconnect with, and reclaim, our deepest and most authentic selves. Why has our search for self always included quiet time in nature?

As did Thoreau, I've experienced nature as life-long companion, reliable guide to my inner truth, and compassionate listener to my toughest questions. In her silence, I've found answers to life's (and my own) greatest mysteries. My deep connection with nature not only provides a continual source of meaning in my life, but also guided this writing.

Years of personal experience (in business, in living my life, in helping others live theirs) have taught me that finding our way home is no more difficult than creating and following a map that actually matches the territory in which we live. We need to realize that it's a map to how we see and think, not a map to more money, status, control or friends. In learning to reframe the *context* of our lives, the *content* of our lives will flow easily, freely and naturally, like a mountain stream in springtime.

To find our way out of the wilderness, we need to recognize, perhaps for the first time, that unconscious adherence to a faulty map, not the demands and chaos of life, got us lost in the first place. It's by seeing things as they truly are, rather than as we think they are (or should be), that we open a path forward. Both full awareness and non-judgmental acceptance of today's current circumstances release the mind from the stranglehold of the past, and actually permit us to see a new way, naturally, with little or no added effort.

Through awareness, we can consciously examine our life context (our map), getting to know *how* we see and think, and with that newfound awareness, create a *new* map, one that allows access to the unlimited potential life has always offered.

It might be useful to think of the transformation in thinking this way: ordinary thinking can get you through an ordinary day, but that same thinking will *stop* you from just about anything "extra-ordinary." If you want to create anything tomorrow that is bigger than what you experienced yesterday, you need a new way of thinking about it.

If you haven't discovered all this on your own, it's probably because you haven't looked. Looking demands that you slow down, and you've been conditioned to believe that slowing down is bad. If I were to trade in a faulty map for a true map, even in wilderness, I could find my way home with confidence and peace. My life would change in an instant.

Knowing now that your true, authentic self lives underneath a tangle of old lessons and beliefs, and knowing that your unconsciously-adopted, habituated thinking is its source, how do you discover the story you've become? Noted animal tracker Tom Brown says when you follow a set of tracks back to its maker, you unravel the mystery of its life story. And when you follow *your own tracks* (the life you experience) back to their maker (the thoughts that created it), you unravel the mystery of *your* life story.

A regular practice of self-reflection offers a level of clarity and perspective uncommon in today's world. With that growing awareness, you'll no longer be able to follow old ways again. My clarity did not come from years of scientific study. As a matter of fact, I tried that, and came up empty. It came from the simple, but dedicated, process of observation, being a student of both my own consciousness and my world. That clarity has offered me more peace and freedom than I ever could have dreamed. This same clarity is available to you.

~~~

"When you follow a set of tracks back to its maker,
you unravel the mystery of its life story."
– Tom Brown, noted animal tracker

~~~

When I've been confronted with any of life's challenges, I've learned, sometimes painfully, not to fight, but to stop, take a step back, and seek first to understand. One question always offers me insight: "What would nature do here?" From early adventures as a young child, to an adult finding peace and connection in nature, to my work as a nature tour leader in some of the world's most pristine wilderness settings, to my coaching and writing, I've found inspiration in nature. With persistence, non-judgment and remarkable consistency, nature tells me:

- to CREATE, with *intention*. Is my life an expression of what matters most to me? What do I hear when I listen for my inner voice? How might I honor the personal truth to which I'm continually drawn?

- to LIVE, with *awareness*. Opportunity depends on uncertainty and change. Possibility shows up in "spaces between," in emptiness. How do I relate to silence? to change? to not knowing? to patience?

- to ACT, with *courage*. Rarely can outcomes be known ahead of time. Can I trust my authentic truth to guide my path in life? How does faith light my way? Might the unknown be my friend?

- to RELATE, with *reverence,* to myself and to others. We're all connected as one. How I think, speak and act profoundly affects my life, as well as the lives of others. Do I live with deep gratitude for all I've been given?

I've always been struck by the clarity and consistency these messages offer. It seems they greet me regardless of situation or topic, independent of the intensity of my request.

When I think about how I'd love to experience my life and work, I envision: resilience and adaptability in the face of uncertainty and complexity, extraordinary creativity and productivity, sustainability, and a deep sense of community. Though perhaps not immediately obvious, nature offers us a perfect archetypal model here—the *ecosystem*. An ecosystem is a dynamic, interdependent community of living things united by common purpose. Ecosystems are home to exceptional creativity and productivity, and have the capability: 1) to create order from uncertainty, 2) to respond to changes within the system by listening to *feedback* (an information flow inherent in all living systems that tells the system how things are going), 3) to learn and adapt in the process, and 4) to build communities of support through cooperation and collaboration. Yet these are the things we seem to fight off, all in the name of control and predictability. How might we learn to see in a new way?

PRACTICE IS THE PATH

Starting quite early, many of us learn that the key to success is to know more and try harder. This may work to pass a test, build a house, or use a computer, but it won't get you to the life of your dreams. If that were possible, you could become an expert skier by reading books on skiing. Or you could learn to live authentically by reading inspirational books. Maybe you've tried! Mastery of anything comes not from knowing, but from the *felt experience* of knowing. To know how to ski, you need to come down the mountain. The mountain teaches you to ski. The same is true if you want to live your truth. Because your thinking determines the reality you experience, the practice here is to develop a *felt experience of your thinking*. Getting to know your thinking takes practice, because rarely are we taught to *notice* our thinking. The promise of my message, therefore, lies not in my words, but in your willingness to try them on, allowing your experience to change you.

We're no strangers to practice. As creatures of habit, almost everything we do is some form of practice. Habits help us master what we do repeatedly. In following an unconscious mental map that doesn't match our lives, however, we've become quite good practicing who we *don't* want to be. Seen this way, your life has been an amazing success; you're an expert at being the person you have practiced so hard to become! You haven't experienced change because you've been practicing *being the same*. If you can get that good at being what you *don't* want, imagine what you could do by practicing what you *do* want.

The obstacle to getting to know your thinking is the unconscious mind. One role of the unconscious is to protect you from danger. But, as an evolutionary adaptation, it sees any kind of change as a threat, not as a possibility; so it doesn't want you to get to know your thinking. Until you interrupt this unconscious flow with conscious awareness, your intention, albeit unconscious, is to keep your thinking small—under the guise of being safe. If you're not living your greatest potential today, it's because, through unconscious habit, you've mastered *not* living it. To get beyond this obstacle, you need to "trick" the unconscious mind. You do that by getting to know it. The conscious mind always has power over the unconscious—but only if you use it—which mostly, we don't. It just takes practice.

A **practice** is an exercise done regularly with an intention of *interrupting* your thinking so as to *get to know* your thinking. As an *observer* of your thoughts, you gain clarity and perspective inaccessible to you as a *participant* in those thoughts. (The participant unconsciously *becomes* the drama and runs down the road with it. The observer instead *notices* all this; and, as such, doesn't get involved in the drama.) When you see your thoughts at work, you learn to trace your thinking back to the assumptions and beliefs that created it. As you do, you see the unconscious nature of your stories and how they've limited you. And as you reflect more deeply on this "*life story of your thinking*," you begin to see how your thinking, not the external world, created those stories.

Can you, as tracker Tom Brown says, follow that habituated thinking back to the "story" that created it, and thereby come to know yourself in a way that sheds light on your "original self?" As you do, you begin to hear the voice of your authentic self. (It's often a quiet voice; it lives in a place of silent awareness; truth doesn't need to yell.) You simply need to become an observer— of your thinking. You don't need to judge how you think, try to change how you think, or re-learn how to think. Just get to know how you *do* think, consciously, maybe for the first time.

Unlike tasks, which have a conclusion, practices are never "done." That's because practices don't force change directly; they nurture the conditions where change occurs naturally.

Compare building a house to tending a garden. You *make* a house; at some point, you're done. With a garden, you *create conditions* conducive to growth—providing water, soil, and sunlight; change happens naturally (you don't *make* roses grow). By nurturing conditions, your old map gets replaced, subtly yet powerfully, by a new map that depicts the true territory of your life. Your truth fills the space created by release of old beliefs.

In a way, self-reflective practice is deceptively simple—*simple* because a six-year-old can "do" it, *deceptive* because all you've learned *since* you were six tells you it can't possibly work.

At the start, it may be confusing to use your thinking to *notice* your thinking. In embracing things rejected by the external world, such as silence, reflection, inquiry, patience, and awareness, you're bound to feel a bit awkward. But you get acquainted with any new place by traveling its roadways repeatedly. Awkwardness disappears through practice. This is where coaches or mentors offer value; they're partners in your practice, so you don't give up when things are uncomfortable.

Let's start, gaining some practice ... with practice. Two basic practices could be life-long additions to your daily ritual, each with the potential to create dramatic change in how you experience life: (1) A practice of personal silence, (2) A practice of observing your thoughts.

A Practice of Personal Silence

Perhaps no more powerful in the journey to transformation, yet at the same time no more misunderstood, is the practice of personal silence. Call it meditation, self-reflection, time-out, prayer, quiet time, or just doing nothing, a regular practice of calming the mind is a pathway into your deepest truth. It's a way to reconnect with your greatest potential. The practice of silence also creates space that opens you to new opportunities, which, although always there, go unnoticed against the backdrop of continual overwhelm and noise that characterizes ordinary life. Insights and answers about life's mystery show up in the gaps between thoughts. If there are no gaps, you may miss this phenomenal source of wisdom altogether, or ignore its messages whenever they manifest. My own experience has taught me that by adopting regular daily quiet time, during which I may calm my mind, observe my thoughts, ponder my pondering, and simply be present in this moment, the world becomes dramatically larger than I ever imagined. The *awareness* I've gained from this practice has expanded into every corner of my life. I don't miss so much; I see more clearly; I see more. Possibilities, connections and patterns show up that I could never know even existed with my mind continuously filled by unconscious automatic "chatter."

As you begin to experience silence, however, you may find yourself feeling resistance, in the form of unconscious messages telling you to revert to the everyday background noise to which you're so habituated. Because we're often taught that being silent means we're unproductive, we fill our lives with noise, then complain about the discomfort of being alone with our own thoughts. Noise is epidemic: phones, media, appliances, kids, adults, music while on hold, video at restaurants and gas stations. Nature, by contrast, exists against a backdrop of silence. Despite the noise a crow can make, it is silent most of the time. A noisy bobcat would fail as a hunter. Trees make little noise as they grow or as they shed their leaves. Although opposite the model we follow, nature displays much of what we'd love—resilience, balance, oneness, peace, integrity, productivity. Perhaps there's a lesson here.

The awareness your mind fights off is the awareness your inner self longs for.

Practice: There's no one right way to be silent except to show up with an intention to do so. For 20 to 30 minutes each day, sit alone in a place free from distraction, a place in nature if possible—ideally, a place you can revisit so as to call it your own. Relax your body, take a few deep breaths. Focus on a simple object in your view. Just be present for the time you choose; no right or wrong. Breathe purposefully; just listen. That's it. If you're in nature, you might listen for her silent messages; she offers all you need to unravel life's mysteries. Invariably, perhaps even for the entire time you're "quiet," you may notice thoughts continually arising, often in the form of inner voices (things to do, chatter, fears). Best you can, acknowledge the thought, let it go, and regain focus. View thoughts as passing clouds; just watch each one as it goes by. Success is being present, not where thoughts take you. Sometimes you will realize you've been lost in a single thought the whole time and haven't quieted your mind at all. Resist judgment; it "just is." Over time, this practice serves to calm your mind. You'll soon notice that your thoughts have been thinking you, rather than you thinking them. (If you don't believe it, try to stop thinking right now. If you're really the one thinking, why can't you stop?) Despite its simplicity and initial awkwardness, this practice reconnects you with soul, spirit, your own deepest truth, life's unity, a higher power, and the center of your existence. Silence focuses awareness on the present moment. That's the moment you *miss* while using your energy to worry about the *next* moment instead. You may find that, through a practice of silence, you feel more confident about yourself and about how you show up in the world, too. As you become intrigued by silence (you will), up the ante: how about no TV, radio, news or malls—for a week? If you feel better (you will), go for another week, then another.

~~~

Stress is a clue—not a problem—telling you it's time to shift ... from "forcing life to happen" to "being keenly aware of this moment," so you can then respond from your own truth.

~~~

A Practice of Observing Your Thoughts

After you've developed some comfort being alone in silence, it's time to shift your gaze inward and get to know your thinking. If you're not consciously aware of your thinking, it's nearly certain that your life is driven by an incessant flow of unconscious, worn-out messages you *think* is thinking. Only by interrupting this flow can you get to know your truth. Using an analogy based on tracking expert Tom Brown's idea, if you follow your own tracks (results) back to their maker (the thoughts that created them), you unravel the mystery of your life story. This practice asks you to slow down, to stop. Contrary to belief, slowing isn't about doing less. It's about not missing so much.

Practice: Stop what you're doing three or four times each day. During a few moments of quiet reflection, replay in your mind thoughts you've had since the last time you stopped. *Listen* to what they tell you. Don't try to change them. Just notice. That's it. Become a student of your thinking. To start, you might identify all the "voices in your head"—more thoughts. With this powerful self-observation practice, you will:

- come to know your thoughts, and grow a *relationship* with them,
- see that only your thoughts determine your experience of reality,
- hear subtle messages of your inner truth,
- distinguish events from the "story" of those events you make up in your mind,
- see life from a broader perspective, *expanding* your world,
- release judgment (as you notice you were the one who created it),
- make conscious choices, easily and naturally,
- discover your unique creative essence, your authentic truth/voice,
- develop the ability to notice your thinking *as* you think,
- come to trust your inner self and truth over the external world.

After a few months of practice with this exercise, you may want to up the ante on your self-reflection by examining the *belief system* that underlies your thinking. Unconsciously-held beliefs drive unconscious thinking. Making them conscious allows you to release outdated ones.

Here's how. During your practice time for observing your thoughts, examine each thought more closely. For example, you may notice a thought such as, "I want to love my work, but there's no way to make a living doing what I love." That's simply a thought! Then stop; ask what old belief may be lurking under the thought. You might discover you'd always been told life is hard, work is harder, and fun comes only after work. You may decide this belief no longer has the power to control your choices. Regular practice opens you to the discovery (and release) of a host of potentially life-constraining beliefs.

As you notice how your thoughts, beliefs and actions are related, you may want to go even deeper and add in the following questions as part of your self-awareness program. How do I know what I know? What constitutes truth? What evidence do I need to know something as true? For things I know to be true, how do I know? (Don't stop until you do know.) This is not about telling you what is true, what to think or what to believe. It's about becoming keenly aware of what truth is to you and getting to know the thinking that brings you to it.

These practices expose you to pressures you face from old lessons that have become obstacles to living authentically. Here's a summary:

- Context is *created* by how you learned to see and think; context is *reinforced* by messages you hear from the world each day. Until you choose your own context, consciously, it's made up by others

- The world doesn't *want* you to change; it wants you to *comply*. Your unconscious mind doesn't want you to change either; it sees anything new and different as *scary*

- If you don't purposefully reclaim the power of your conscious mind, you could live your entire life from programmed belief

- Your authentic self *thrives* on change, uncertainty, the unknown

- Your conscious mind is your *agent*, both for connecting with your authentic self and for making a huge shift in your perspective

- *Remaining* conscious takes continual *practice*

- Practice works by giving you felt experience of your truth; the *felt experience* changes you—so *you* don't have to; you naturally step into choosing a context of possibility that lets you live your truth

Your well-learned and probably well-developed "skill" at fighting with life may have offered the illusion of success—when life was simpler. You remember those times, right? What worked for you then may very likely lead to failure now. The reason you struggle is that you've not learned to trust yourself. More specifically, you've learned to *not* trust yourself. The stress you may feel today isn't a problem; it's a *clue*, telling you it's time to shift ... from "controlling life's outcomes" to "being keenly aware of this moment." This level of consciousness allows you to then respond from your own truth, rather than react to life's external circumstances. This is a world of self-trust.

Note: The unconscious mind will keep saying: (1) oh, that looks easy, (2) if I just 'do' it, I'll be done, (3) it makes sense, so I must already get it. Not so. We love the *idea* that rational knowing can change us, but practices are not tasks. You don't *do* practices; you *become* them—through deep personal experience. Felt experience changes you. How long does it all take? As long as it takes for you to let go of the stories that hold you back today ... which depends on your *noticing* those stories as nothing more than noisy tenants in your mind. It's amazing how much space you free up when the voices go calm. *In this empty space*, your truth emerges. There are no textbooks here; you're using your *experience* of yourself to *discover* your authentic self.

For all your practices, you'll find it beneficial to adopt a practice of journaling. After each session, write about your experience. Note what came up. You might ask yourself: What did I *feel*? What did I *think* (a thought underlying, and therefore evoking, the feeling)? How are my feelings and thoughts related? How do they relate to choices I make? No need to make anything or anyone right or wrong, to change anything or judge anything you see. Whatever shows up teaches you. Write it down.

~~~

"We make our world significant by the courage of our questions and by the depth of our answers."
– Carl Sagan

~~~

AN INVITATION

There are many pathways that lead to discovering your authentic self, just as there are many roads to get from your home to a favorite picnic spot. So, too, with finding and living your truth. Each of us is different, so we respond to ideas in our own unique ways. I offer three distinct paths, each shining a different light onto your journey to self, each with its own set of ideas and practices, each with a perspective designed to connect you with your innate creative essence:

- **Authentic Communication:** we live life through the lens of language, "in conversation." ***Constructive Conversations*** (Chapter 4) creates a path to your authentic truth designed around the idea that when your *communication* is authentic, *you* are authentic.

- **Authentic Connection:** we are part of nature; although we've often forsaken this sacred connection. ***In Nature's***

Image (Chapter 5) creates a path to your authentic truth designed around the idea that by connecting with this universal truth, you become *your own* truth.

- **Authentic Presence:** we are beings of consciousness; our thinking creates reality. *Personal Responsibility* (Chapter 6) offers a path to your authentic truth designed around the idea that through awareness of your thinking, you trust yourself—in each moment … *becoming* your true self.

There's no right or best path—just the one that works for you. (I admit to loving all three.) Start with one whose title speaks to you. Follow where it may lead. Then, perhaps as a way to deepen your journey, try another. The scenery on each differs, but they all take you *home*—to who you've always been.

~~~

"There's nothing in a caterpillar that tells
you it's going to be a butterfly."
– Buckminster Fuller

~~~

Living Authentically
... in a World That Would Rather You Didn't

Part II

Pathways to Your Unique Truth

Chapter 4

Authentic Communication

Constructive Conversations

"The single biggest problem in communication is
the illusion that it has taken place."

— George Bernard Shaw

INTRODUCTION

Imagine what it would be like if you could make every conversation you had, with anyone (including yourself), about any topic (including contentious ones), both *constructive and satisfying*. You can.

Imagine what it would be like if instead of feeling stressed or threatened, you felt *confident and at ease*, about all your communication, spoken or written, regardless of circumstances. You can.

Imagine what it would be like if you had the clarity and perspective to handle every conversation with *reverence and grace*, personally and professionally. You can.

This chapter is entitled **Constructive Conversations**; its intent is to help you make all your conversations constructive, for *you*, regardless of subject, players, stakes, skill or emotion—by evoking capacities already living inside you. There are many pathways to "living authentically." Through the lens of your communication is one of the more powerful ones. As with other pathways, this assumes you have completed "The Basics" portion of the Living Authentically program beforehand.

We live our lives "in conversation," whether with friends, family, managers, store clerks, customers, phone support people, even ourselves. We experience every aspect of life—how we believe, see, think, speak and act—through the lens of language. It's our most powerful tool for making fundamental change in the course of our lives. Yet for all the potential language holds to create possibility, rarely do we either learn or experience its phenomenal power.

Some conversations go well; some don't. Why? You might blame the circumstances; some situations are just difficult. Yet *you* are not your circumstances. You might blame your level of skill. Yet it's the same *you* in both. What makes a conversation constructive also makes a conversation unconstructive. It's called **context**. Context has nothing to do with the **content** of the conversation. (I'll explore content a bit later.) Context is an invisible framework *surrounding* your conversations (and your relationships, and work, and vacations, and life), made up of **how you see and think** about them. Until you become aware of it, context is the residual product of old lessons, unexamined assumptions, false beliefs, outdated viewpoints—and the bad habits they generate—which both appear as reality and *block* your *natural* awareness and ability. Difficult conversations are difficult only because *you* made them so ... unknowingly, of course, by how you think about them. As long as you're unaware this is so, you feel, and are, powerless to effect change.

You are a *natural* communicator; you always have been. Stop for a moment; notice your reaction to that statement. Did you say to yourself, "yeah right, but that's not true for *me*?" If so, that idea is a **thought**, and it's an example of how the way you *think* about conversations changes who you *are* in conversations. By seeing things this way, you give your power to the beliefs living in your unconscious mind, leaving them in charge of how you approach conversations. Your natural effectiveness is already inside you. You need only release the thinking that blocks it, thinking you've unwittingly adopted (and practiced) for many years.

Here are a few examples of bad lessons you may have learned over the years, lessons now embedded in your unconscious mind as "truth."

- I'm not good at communicating; some people are, but not me
- Conflict is normal; I must either learn to avoid it or to fight it
- If I speak my truth, people won't like me
- Force and control get things done better than calm presence
- If I make a mistake, it means I failed, so I won't risk it
- Life is supposed to be difficult

And because you believe they're true, you not only honor them, but rarely stop to question them. It's as if old lessons have created a cloud in front of you, obscuring your vision, filtering your thinking, and blocking your natural awareness and ability, all without your consent. Both the possibility you seek and the potential you represent—the world without these assumptions and lessons—live on the other side of the cloud. Yet the cloud appears to be real, so you believe you're stuck. Worse, because of this illusion, you wouldn't believe that the cloud is made up in your head, a result of old ways of seeing and thinking. The cloud is made visible only by the shadow it casts in your life ... the struggles you experience, the stress and anxiety you feel, the challenge life has become. Yet your mind doesn't draw any connection between the two. Resolution, therefore, won't come from developing new skills, or from changing either life or its circumstances, for none of these is the problem. With clarity of perception and broader perspective—***conscious awareness***—the cloud vanishes.

Stop here for a few minutes of reflection. Sit quietly and think about your conversations today. How would you assess your communications effectiveness? You may see yourself as competent in some areas, and perhaps less so in others. For example, you may believe you communicate effectively at work but not in your relationships, or that you communicate more naturally when things are going well than in times of conflict. This exercise is a crucial step in learning to live and communicate authentically. Journal your reflections. Complete, non-judgmental acceptance of what's true today is the greatest power you have to create meaningful change tomorrow. The right answer is what's true for *you*.

Over the years, I've asked my clients to speak to how they'd *like* to be able to communicate in the future, ways that are *not* true for them today. Here's a sample of their responses. Notice what each evokes in you:

- I'm non-judgmental in how I listen and speak

- I treat others with respect, even if I disagree with them
- I've made a personal commitment to being constructive
- I make clear, powerful, and compelling requests, with ease
- I offer unconditionally constructive feedback to others
- I feel authentic in my communication, evidenced by lack of stress, discomfort, or fear of uncertainty
- My personal culture is curiosity; every situation is a teacher
- I consciously choose my intention in each moment
- I'm aware of exactly *how* I'm listening and speaking; I'm aware of the same in others, too. I therefore know how I am being heard.
- I believe there are many right answers to every challenge
- I have extreme clarity on what's important to me and what's not
- I use my clarity and perspective to make life work for me
- I'm "emotionally intelligent;" I *have* feelings, but I don't *become* them; therefore, they don't cloud my perception
- I trust myself
- I believe every one of us represents unlimited possibility
- I don't choose an outcome or agenda beforehand; I have no need to control others; I trust the conversation will show me the way.

Each of these is a powerful, yet *natural,* result of learning to see and think in new ways, not a result of acquiring new skills. Each is realized simply by expanding context, how you see and think. None depend on the situation, or on the content of your communication. Each depicts a place "beyond the cloud" of illusion.

Read the list again, this time imagining yourself *being* the person each statement describes. What would life be like for you if these statements were true for you? Just imagine ... for now.

The Significance of Context

Little of this book is about the details, or *content* of your conversations. Even the end of this chapter touches only minimally on content. That's because content isn't the problem. In fact, what you want to say in a conversation barely makes the top ten list of things to think about. The focus here is the *thought framework* within which details happen.

Not only is 90% of this book about context, 90% of your effectiveness in life is about context, too, even though today you may not see it that way. Further, I suspect that 90% of the breakdowns, failures and problems you have—both in life and in communicating—are about context, not content. I also claim that if you learn to devote your energy to being aware of, and purposefully choosing, the *context* of your conversations (and life), the *content* of your conversations (and life) will flow with meaning, power and grace—all on their own, naturally.

Constructive conversations are *authentic* conversations. No substitutes. This means getting to know your own unique truth and choosing to live in complete trust of it. Your authentic truth may have been left dormant, possibly for years, under a shroud of unconsciously held assumptions and beliefs about how you need to be someone else instead. Self-trust is perhaps *the* key criterion for effective communication. It's tempting to think you can "pretend to be authentic" and get away with it. Although it's easy to fake your words, you can't fake self-trust. But if you can learn to be 100% real, why would you even want to? When you trust yourself, you no longer need to know outcomes ahead of time, control others, have agendas, be backed into a corner by the behavior of others, or censor your presence.

When we think of conversations, it's common to think "transactions," back-and-forth exchanges between people, with a primary, yet often-unstated, agenda held by both parties to get their way. The problem with this approach is that, even before beginning, context is so small there's not much space for new ideas to show up. When we've focused ahead of time on there being only one outcome—how we get our way—there's often one winner and one loser. Possibility is limited.

Effective conversations are *transformations*, not transactions. They ask for bigger thinking, mutual respect, shared intention, belief in many right answers, active listening, true dialogue, willingness to learn and be changed in the process, emotional intelligence, personal responsibility, and extreme awareness— of self, other, environment. All are part of creating a larger contextual framework; none depend upon the topic itself.

PRINCIPLES AND PRACTICES FOR EXCEPTIONAL CONVERSATIONS

So, what makes up this invisible framework, or context, and how does it have such impact on conversations—negative or positive? I've identified five elements of context, all of which are 100% within your ability to choose (or control, if you like). Each can manifest *unconsciously*, from old lessons and beliefs, the cause of ineffective communication, or *consciously*, from your authentic truth, the natural communicator inside you. You "shift" your presence from one to the other through the practice of getting to know the thinking that created your current context—your old unconscious ways. As you make old ways conscious, they then disappear naturally, creating space for the authentic you to emerge. Your growing **awareness** is the catalyst for change.

As you become a master of *context*, that of your own consciousness as well as that of the conversation itself, then the *content*, or details, of those conversations simply take care of themselves—often so well, it turns out, that *you* no longer have to. This is one of the true sources of power offered by developing conscious awareness of your thinking.

These same five elements of context frame every conversation, whether it's idle chat, business communication, conflict resolution, dreaming about an amazing future, or even internal self-talk. For each element, you will find both explanatory material (how that element contributes to the success or failure of a conversation), and practical material (how you can integrate new ideas into your ways of being) so your conversations are far more effective and you are far more authentic.

You make your *conversations* constructive (i.e. authentic) by making *yourself* constructive (i.e. authentic). You do that via "simple" everyday practices of becoming aware of your thinking. Through these practices, your authentic self emerges (or better said, re-emerges), naturally.

The practices suggested for each element of context build upon the foundation practices you've already adopted—(1) a practice of silence, and (2) a practice of observing your thinking. The benefit to this approach is that, as you add an exercise for each new topic to your daily practice, you'll be building a single, integrated practice of self-awareness that offers all you need to become the communicator (and authentic self) you wish to be.

As a recap, here's a summary of those two basic practices:

Personal silence: Perhaps no more powerful in the journey to transformation, yet no more misunderstood, is a practice of personal silence. A regular practice of calming the mind is a pathway to your deepest truth and greatest potential. Sit quietly, alone for 20 to 30 minutes each day. Relax your body, take a few deep breaths. Focus on a simple object in your view. Breathe purposefully; just listen. Be present; there's no right or wrong. You'll likely find thoughts continually arising, often in the form of inner voices (things to do, fears, etc.) View them as passing clouds; just watch each as it goes by. Silence focuses your awareness on the present moment. That's the moment you tend to *miss* while you're using your energy to worry about the *next* moment instead.

Observe your thoughts: If you're not aware of your thinking, life is driven by an incessant flow of unconscious voices you *think* is thinking. Only by interrupting this flow will you know your truth. As an *observer* of your thoughts, you gain a perspective on your consciousness you'd never get as a *participant* alone. When you see your thoughts at work, you can trace them back to the old assumptions, beliefs and lessons that created them. This allows you to choose new beliefs. *Stop* what you're doing three or four times a day. During a few moments of quiet reflection, replay in your mind thoughts you've had since the last replay, as if a movie with you as its audience. *Listen* to what they tell you. Resist judging or trying to change them. Just notice.

Each practice suggested in the pages ahead asks you to create 15 to 20 minutes of dedicated personal time each day. Each follows the format of the basic practices above and is designed to enhance self-discovery by exposing the unconscious stories that underlie your thinking for that element of communications context. During your quiet reflective time, replay in your mind several situations, events and conversations from your day. Include some that went well, some that didn't, even conversations you had with yourself. In your replay (now), notice your thinking (then). By tracing your behavior back to the thinking that created it, you see how old, unconscious thinking forms the invisible framework surrounding your entire experience of life, coloring what you know as "reality," often inhibiting your true self. With practice, you become deeply aware of your consciousness. That awareness alone causes your thinking to change, naturally, evoking the authentic "you." No need to judge or change what you discover; it's about learning. You will find it helpful to journal what you discover.

I. INTERPRETATION

Many things happen to you over the course of a day. Then there's *how you think* about things that happen. Interpretation is the story you tell, and it can often run far astray from the reality of events themselves. Without conscious awareness, interpretation is an auto-pilot response to life, driven by the unconscious mind—which sees the world through old lessons. In its desire to defend you from danger, it creates threats, even when they don't exist. Over time, this causes you to not live life, but to live a *story* about life. Think of interpretation as a life story of your **thinking**, not the life story of your life. Life's events rarely cause trouble; *interpretations* do. When you're unaware of the "spin" you put on events, (or even that you're doing it!) you're likely to see your response as part of the event itself, thereby justifying your action. But as you become *aware* of how your thinking works, and that your reaction to an event is separate from the event itself, you release interpretation entirely. Some *ineffective* (unconsciously chosen) interpretations: taking things personally, believing you're not good enough, thinking life should be fair, believing there can be only one right answer, or that *your* answer is the right one. An *effective* interpretation could be: things happen; what's possible now?

You might think of **interpretation** as "how you've got life figured out." You've had years of practice seeing the world through this lens of early lessons and experiences, which now act as a filter, altering your perception—of yourself, others, life. Life's events, situations and happenings are almost always neutral; alone, they carry little emotional charge. How you've come to experience them, however, may be just the opposite.

A simple example: another driver pulls sharply in front of you on the highway. That's an event. Things happens; no big deal, right? "Well, I'll *tell* you what: he's an idiot; he did it on purpose; he did it *to me*. It's personal." That's *interpretation*. The event itself is neutral; it asks only that you slow down so as to not hit the other car. Your angered response comes not from the event, but from the *story* you told yourself about the event. Your story is interpretation, and it's a choice you make—even if you don't see it as a choice today. For almost any event in life, there is rarely hard evidence to validate interpretation. Unaware this is happening, you can't simply choose differently. You instead respond in anger, and perhaps (at least if you live in Massachusetts) speed up, pass him, then jam on your brakes.

Today, it's more likely that you believe your reaction to be part of the event itself; perhaps you can't imagine "letting someone get away with that kind of thing on the roads." Because you see both "as one"—the event and your response—the world often feels like a hostile place, as you place blame on others for all the insanity in your life.

You release interpretation by learning to recognize thoughts that drive it. If you *knew* you were making up stuff in your head, chances are good you'd change your "mind." I don't know many people who knowingly would limit their lives by making up stories. I do, however, know people who, through lack of awareness alone, feel justified in their anger.

Generalizing this example, "things happen" all the time. It's the way life is. Over the course of a day, *hundreds* of things happen. They include things you think and say, things you do, things you notice about others, how others treat you, things others say and do, things you see on TV or on the way to work. You generally don't get to *choose* what happens, including the behavior of others. What you *can* choose, however, is how you *see* what happens. Everything that happens in the course of your day is a candidate for interpretation; each offers you a choice.

As you learn to distinguish between "the way it is" (events) and your "story" about the way it is (interpretation), you teach yourself how to respond only to "what is," releasing the life-constraining thinking and judgment that comes from your story. You do this by learning to consciously notice your thinking, the thinking that *creates* your story. As you do, your story begins to fade, and you begin to see a much bigger and more peaceful world, create new possibility for yourself, have amazingly productive conversations, and save a ton of energy that you can use for more worthwhile pursuits—like your biggest dreams. It is in this sense that interpretation is the core, not just of effective communication, but of almost every aspect of living authentically: resilience, balance, peace, meaning, satisfaction, relationships, career, joy.

Here are some interpretations common in our world today. Unaware, we rarely see the impact these have on our behavior, largely because we can't even imagine we've created the problems in the first place.

- I have to be right, in control
- I'm always wrong, a victim
- I have to be nice so I don't hurt anyone
- I have to be mean if I want to get things done
- I have to be responsible, for myself, others, life, everything
- I have to be tough so they won't see the fears inside me
- I have to prove myself, so I can be "good enough"
- Life/they/the world should be fair/easy/go my way

With each of these interpretations, an old lesson, experience or belief has been unconsciously "evoked" into your way of being. As an adult, you *defend* this false self, behaving so as to prove your interpretation, to yourself and to others. Over the years, "practicing" this interpretation became your "winning strategy." You've now come to rely on this approach for all of life's situations; you claim your success as evidence of its truth; you've even come to believe this is who you really are.

As a child, I learned I had to "get things right." The way I interpreted this was that if got A's, I'd be worthy of love. I grew up to be an adult known for getting things right. I even believed that's who I was. After all, I'd had all this "success" with it. Needless to say, I left behind me a wake of people I'd hurt over those years. The business world loved and rewarded me for this behavior ... to about the same level that my relationships detested it; after all, spouses don't often appreciate "being fixed." Here I left yet another wake behind me.

You have a prevailing interpretation, and you have a winning strategy. They're the *unconscious* result of how and what you learned early in life. At the moment, however, you may not be aware they exist, so you can't know how they limit you. You probably *do* know that "the way you are" helps you succeed. As is true with any kind of life change, the path forward is simple observation. By coming to recognize your interpretation as illusion, you begin to see yourself for who and what you really are, *without* the "interpretation." Gradually, you come to release parts of you that don't serve you. It may sound paradoxical, yet the act of noticing judgment is non-judgmental. It's the noticing that causes the judgment to fall away.

Until you get to this point, however, you limit new possibility to what interpretation has already created for you. If you're content to keep fixing stuff that's wrong, maybe you don't care. As for me, my heart ached for all I'd lost; I chose to notice. As you observe your thoughts, you may even see how you've become resentful that the world doesn't appreciate who you are and all you've achieved through your strategy. As the depth of your inquiry continues, you may see that your resentment is actually directed toward *yourself*, for having traded away your true self in order to gain approval from others (approval you probably never got anyway). As the inquiry delves deeper still, you may realize that the only limitation in your life was the one you laid on yourself—by looking to others for what was inside you all along. And it's at this point that life begins to flow peacefully. Notice, from this description, the true power of looking more and more deeply into your own ways of being.

Perhaps the greatest obstacle we face in life—the reason life feels like such a struggle for so many—is our inability to see, then accept, "what is." Because we identify ourselves with our interpretation, we see life, and ourselves, as we *think* they are, not as they *truly* are. Society loves that we do this, because when we don't think for ourselves, consciously, we're easier prey for going along with the thinking of others instead.

Everyone has different histories and experiences, so everyone's "ways of being" differ. We're all the same ... just in different ways. The unconscious mind may always see these differences as threats, yet as you learn to *interrupt* its incessant flow of interpretation using the conscious mind, you begin to see how *your* life created the person *you* are today, just as *their* life created who *they* are today, too. Not wrong, just different. To get to know someone, however, through the lens of *understanding* rather than the lens of *judgment*, leads naturally to the place of acceptance, even if you don't agree with them. And with acceptance comes an opening to constructive conversations and personal peace.

Why do we allow our "thinking" to lead us to falsehoods we accept as *truth*, with none of the inquiry, critical thinking or conversation upon which *truth* depends? My opinion: the unconscious perceives safety in *predictability.* So we'd rather accept the false as truth than to live with uncertainty. We believe what we *want* to believe, regardless of evidence. That's the root of interpretation. Its opposite is *discernment*—the *conscious* thought process used to distinguish truth from falsehood, to distinguish life's facts and events (which simply exist) from opinions we have about them. As we make this distinction, the "negative energy" in interpretation also begins to fall away, leaving peace in its stead.

Interpretation: A Practice of Releasing Judgment. As you replay the day's situations, events and conversations, name the *event* (as others would report it), then your *interpretation* of the event, (the story you told yourself about why it mattered *to you*). Notice the differences. Then name *feelings* you experienced, and *actions* you took. Lastly, see if you can trace feelings and actions more to interpretation than to the event itself. After some practice with this, look for a "habitual prevailing interpretation" that drives your behavior across most of life. Common answers: I'm right; I'm wrong; I'm afraid; life should... Once you find this foundation of your life context, you're free to choose a new one, one that leads to clarity of thought and release of judgment. *Advanced practice*: once each day, pledge to "tell and live a new story," fueled by a belief that the *story you tell* becomes the *story you live.*

II. INTENTION

No matter what kind of conversation you have, it's likely that you have a desired outcome in mind. What you may *not* have in mind, however, is *conscious awareness* of that "desire." And here, once again, is where the unconscious mind hijacks your desires. Without conscious awareness and clarity of what you desire, the unconscious mind chooses one for you—with neither your awareness nor consent. Its role is to keep you out of danger, which it does by peddling old beliefs and lessons, choosing so as to defend you whenever it feels tension. In this way, your intention is not only unknown to you, but may well result in your getting just what you *don't* want. You might think of the issue here as "*intention deficit disorder.*" Let's face it: you choose intention consciously all the time ... in conversations that are "easy." You fail when things get in the *way* of what's natural: emotion, fear, high stakes, unconscious thinking. Often unaware when these things creep in, it's easy to miss altogether the chance to take responsibility for how it goes. The last thing you'd "intend" is to show up defensively when you're in a conversation where collaborative resolution means a great deal to you. The problem here is that the unconscious cares about the **risk** in the matter, not the **possibility** in the matter. Possibility lives *outside* the box your unconscious is trying to keep you *inside.*

You might think of **intention** as "what you're up to" in a conversation. You're always up to something, but rarely are you fully aware of what that *something* is—which means it can change in an instant, when things get sidetracked, when emotions loom large, when the subject changes, or when you (or another) begin to take things personally. None of these contribute to effective conversations or to constructive results. Of course, as before, you change all this by becoming consciously aware of your thinking, and, with that awareness, choosing an intention that matches what you "truly" want, by drawing on mutual respect, reciprocity and reverence. Examples of *ineffective* (unconsciously chosen) intentions include to win, blame, be right, defend. Examples of *effective* intentions: to learn, understand, create, help, serve, resolve. Either way, intention is a reflection of who you are being in the moment. Intention is a powerful language construct because it evokes energy *inside* you to create a new world *outside* you.

Have you ever entered a conversation intending to resolve an issue with peace and ease, only to have things turn into a heated argument instead? At one time or another, most of us have. And when this happens, do you find that you blame the other person for the breakdown? At one time or another, most of us have. What's often happening is that you *think* you want one thing from the conversation, yet you *behave* in a way that gets you something else. You're not consciously aware this is happening, so you miss the signals that changed the game.

Example: You're talking with your spouse, perhaps of dreams for your child's education. The conversation is full of potential; it's going well. You use the child's science project as an example; something triggers your spouse. Maybe you didn't get poster board in time. Now you're being attacked for screwing up. Intention just changed, and at least one of you missed it. The revised intention is to make you wrong. Unaware, you get defensive. Now *your* intention changed, too. A fight ensues.

Awareness alone can change this. Had either of you been *consciously* aware of your intention to discuss the possibility your child's education holds, you could have noticed the shift *as it occurred*, avoiding things devolving into argument. In that new moment, you might have chosen either: (1) to bring the subject back to the intended one, or (2) to respond to the "issue" without any personal attachment or judgment, and then move on. The problem here is not the other person, (even if they truly are wrong!) but lack of conscious awareness—*clarity of intention*.

The world's great masters "got this." What *made* them masters was that they held their intention so strongly that nothing could deter them. Examples include Gandhi (unconditional dignity),

Jesus (clarity of heart, unconditional love), the Buddha (clarity of thought), Mother Teresa (unconditional service), Martin Luther King (unconditional respect), Steve Jobs (elegant design). How might *you* be a master? An old saying suggests: "Seek not the masters; seek what the masters sought." What they sought was a level of conscious awareness that allowed them to sustain their intention more strongly that most of us can even imagine.

Intention: A Practice of Gaining Clarity. As you replay the day's situations, events and conversations, notice (now) the thinking and perspective you had (then), and how they helped form your *intention*—what you "wanted" from the situation or conversation. Notice how your intention then impacted your behavior. Notice also how *aware* of this you were in that moment. As the relationship between awareness and intention becomes clearer to you, envision how specific conversations might have gone differently had you been more aware, and had you therefore made different choices. Without judgment, see if you can demonstrate to yourself that *every* conversation actually goes just as you "intend," even if intention was chosen unconsciously—from old habits. *Advanced practice*: listen "through the noise" to hear the passion of your heart, energy that wants to express itself through how you live.

III. EMOTION

Prevailing wisdom suggests that emotions happen "spontaneously," which therefore makes them valid, thereby justifying any reaction or outburst. More likely, the exact opposite is true. Feelings come largely from unconscious thoughts. Emotions are life's great *teachers*, carrying messages that ask you to stop, listen and learn, often about your own thinking. Yet by being unaware, or *ineffective*, you don't *want* to stop, listen and learn. A common tactic to avoid personal responsibility is pretending that emotions qualify as *evidence* for your reaction. And if emotions are screaming for attention, you can't connect meaningfully with others. When you *get to know* the thinking that drives emotion (clue: interpretation), you become *effective*, or "emotionally intelligent."

You may have been taught to think of *"**emotional intelligence**"* as a measure of how well you *manage* or *control* emotions. I see it a very different way: you are emotionally intelligent when you *have* emotions, (allowing them to serve as teachers), but choose not to *become* them (so they no longer cloud the clarity of your perception). Viewed this way, emotional intelligence has a huge impact on communicating effectively, because centeredness and perceptual clarity are so crucial.

The role emotions play in our lives is as teachers. They could care less about our drama or reactions. They simply want us to learn—about ourselves, others, life. Feelings arise from our conditioned response to life, a result of interpretation— *unconscious thoughts* we hold about how life should be. As we learn to cherish feelings for their learning value, we become emotionally intelligent and better communicators. For example, *guilt* arises from thinking we're not good enough, a habitual response to years of bad lessons. If we didn't hold that thought, we'd not feel guilty. We'd reserve guilt for big things, like purposefully hurting someone.

Much of our struggle with communicating effectively comes from our inability to separate thoughts and feelings—*having* feelings but not *becoming* them, as well as misreading this emotional context in others. As a result, our conversations are often driven by emotion, just at the point when we want them to be driven by rational thought.

By having learned that emotions give us a right to judge or react, we've commonly adopted one of three *equally ineffective* responses to our emotions: avoid/deny (silence), control/fight (violence), or dramatics (*become* the emotion). We even name some people as avoiders, as confronters, as acceptors, and as drama queens. Having chosen one of these "prevailing strategies," we see any other approach as undesirable compromise, which serves to keep us attached to our prevailing response.

The problem here is that *all three* approaches deny the *learning* that emotions offer; this leaves *emotions* in charge of our conversations, not us. And because we often believe the path forward is for *someone else* to change, emotions persist, becoming a primary influence in our lives.

Emotions in the workplace have taken an especially bad rap. As a result, we learn to suppress both the emotion and our *innate* emotional intelligence. Yet *truth* is carried by emotional energy, not just by words. We live and work naturally from the underlying truth of emotional energy.

Key points about your relationship with your emotional self:

- Emotions don't come from what happens, but from *interpretation*—how you *see and think* about what happens.

- Because you're *unaware* of how you see and think, you don't know your response isn't truly your own.

- The unconscious tries to protect you from perceived consequences of fears it learned ages ago, not to help you create a positive future.

- You develop emotional intelligence by *getting to know your feelings, then getting to know the thoughts that drive them.*

- When you *know* your thinking, trust replaces old belief.

- Emotional intelligence is *not* about controlling emotions; it's about learning from their messages, and the thinking that underlies them.

- As you learn to distinguish between "*having* an emotion" and "*becoming* an emotion;" your *relationship* with emotions improves.

- As you come to treat *yourself* the way you'd like others to treat you, your connections deepen markedly—with yourself, others, and life.

Emotion: A Practice of Honoring Feelings. Using the practice from the interpretation section, focus your replay on *emotions* you experienced in each event or situation. Carefully trace each **feeling** back to the **thinking** that created it. Example: A feeling: I'm angry. An interpretation: She *made* me angry. But ... with deeper inquiry, you may discover that *you made yourself* angry, because you felt that you weren't good enough in some way and were afraid to expose that. It's critical to trace feelings back as far as you can, because their underlying cause is invariably *within you*, not about someone else. You may now choose a new belief: I am good enough. New beliefs/thoughts cause old feelings to fade. You now honor your feelings, rather than either deny them or become them. *Advanced practice*: Notice the "consciousness level" you *chose* to respond to an event: drama (who can I blame?), facts (what happened?), principle (who do I want to be?), potential (what's possible here?).

IV. Listening

When it comes to listening, it seems we'd prefer not to. What we generally call listening is, more accurately, planning what we're going to say when the other person is done talking. In unconscious, *ineffective* listening, you don't truly listen, you listen **for**. You listen *for* threats to your comfort zone (what you already know), and for what you *think should be* rather than what *truly is*. Both are interpretations, not listening, and put you and your communication on the defense. Instead, *effective* or conscious listening carries with it an intention to learn, not judge. When you learn to separate your opinion from what's being said, you become open to new learning. Research shows that words make up only 7% of what you hear; most of a message comes from voice tone, intuition, body language and energy presence. With practice, you learn to hear what's *not* being said, including the conflicting messages often present when words, intuition and energy don't match. Realizing that listening is not the same as agreeing, you begin to release judgment.

As a society, we favor answers over questions, busyness over silence, expedience over completeness, and often, drama over meaning. None of these encourages listening. We *say* we want meaning, peace and satisfaction both in how we communicate and in life, yet we're often unwilling to practice the deeper reflection upon which these things depend.

The implication is simple: we don't listen; we listen "for." We listen *for* that which reinforces what we already believe; so we *interpret* rather than *hear*. Instead of absorbing what *they said*, we hear a story of how it supports or diminishes what *we believe*. Unconsciously, we look for threats to our comfort zone, the "edges" of what we know. To listen this way not only blocks openness to anything new but causes us to miss the depth of what others have to offer.

A simple example: Stop for a minute and check in with your listening; notice how you're listening to the words here. If you find you're listening by asking, "What can I find wrong with what he's saying?" I promise you won't be disappointed. If you find you're listening by asking, "What possibility might he offer me?" I promise you won't be disappointed either. You hear what you listen for. To truly listen, you first have to be willing to be *changed* by what you hear; you do this by letting go of your interpretation. You'll never hear the voices of others if your own voice is screaming for attention.

How we listen is not about words alone. Research shows that only 7% of a message comes from words. 38% of what we hear comes from emotion and voice tone, and 55% comes from energy, presence and intuition. So, when you claim you've heard the words, you can be missing up to 93% of what's being "said."

As you learn to listen fully, you hear "complete messages," from others and *from yourself,* by integrating words, voice tone, emotion, body language, presence and energy. As you do, your awareness picks up mismatches—where words don't match voice tone, where intention doesn't match emotion. You do much of this today. It's how you know you don't trust someone (or yourself). You "hear" the mismatch between their words and their body language. Anyone can make up *words* to get you to see things their way. It's far more difficult to "pretend" energy, presence, or voice tone. As a listener, you'll be able to hear it all, uncluttered by interpretation.

As you become practiced at listening deeply, you also begin to connect more deeply with the reality of others. For in order to appreciate a deep connection with another, you need to get beyond your own "story," (and theirs), and connect with something inside you that "gets" what's going on inside them. Without this combination of depth and freedom, judgment and emotion (yours *and* theirs) will block your understanding. And to emphasize, listening is about understanding and learning, not about your response. Temptation to add your opinion or to offer advice are not part of listening.

The answers and guidance we need in order to make our conversations constructive are already *inside* the conversations. When we calm the chatter of interpretation and emotion, we release unconscious judgment, allowing us to hear the guidance. Only by hearing it can we follow it.

In summary, listening is a two-way, non-judgmental and agenda-free process of understanding, conducted in an environment of mutual respect and openness.

Listening: A Practice of Hearing Deeply. During your replay, look at how you may have listened *for*, rather than just listened, and how this interpretation/judgment impacted what you heard, and in turn, what you said or did. Notice how judgment may have created a protective stance. Then, replay again, now seeking to discover non-verbal aspects—yours as well as the others'. What did you "hear" from emotional context, intuition, body language, voice, energy? Did they all "match?" How did the match (or not) affect how you heard the "big picture" story, as well as your sense of trust? ***Advanced practice***: pledge to listen only to learn. Release the need to judge, change, control. Listen for presence, energy, emotion. Allow the intuitive mind to hear what the rational mind cannot.

V. PERSONAL RESPONSIBILITY

When you act from the unconscious, *ineffective*, mind, "you" are a reflection of your old defensive beliefs. This conditioned self is more worried about protecting its edges than in learning or growing. Conversations mirror your lack of self-confidence. The path to *effective* communication is personal authenticity. As you become aware of your thoughts, consciously, your authentic self emerges, without effort.

By releasing your stories, agendas, goals, need to manage others, or worry about outcomes, you'll become free to allow your true self to set clear intention, then non-judgmentally "listen your way" through every conversation you have, hearing the natural feedback already ***in*** the conversation as a guide to your path forward. Your conversations become guided by *principles*—the kind of person you choose to be. Personal clarity is a powerful tool for building **capacities** that serve you everywhere in life—*resilience, discernment, adaptability, creativity*. These attributes are far different from our all-too-common strategies of command and control. If you're not coming from your own authentic truth, you're come from someone else's. Living from your authentic self means *no-one* can take your power away from you.

You make your *conversations* authentic by making *yourself* authentic. And you do that by *getting to know* your thinking, so you can release all the "thinking" that isn't truly your own. It's curious to think that you *create* whatever you experience today as reality—through the clarity and consciousness of your thinking. All along, you probably believed life (and some people) are just difficult. "Real reality" is that all of life is a perfect reflection of the *thinking* with which you approach it. If your life isn't a reflection of what you'd *like* it to be, or what you *thought* it would be, then change your thinking. That's actually the point of this entire book. As you become your true self, a self who has always been inside you, your innate nature as an effective communicator will re-emerge as well. After all, it's who you really are!

A client asked me recently why the conversations he and I have are so constructive, while many of his others are not. My answer: **personal responsibility**. We *choose* that our conversations be that way. When you choose to be your true self, you regain a huge amount of energy in life, because you no longer need to remember "who you're trying to be."

One person is responsible for making your conversations constructive; that person is *you*. If you don't like how *you* are behaving, *you* can make new choices. If you don't like how *they* are behaving, *you* can make new choices. Yes—it is all about you. You can choose what you believe, see, think, say and do in every moment, even if you're tired, scared or angry. This may sound like a huge task to take on. It's not. It's a small task with big impact. Although you may not discover it until you choose to do it, you'll find that by claiming full responsibility for how your conversations and your life go, you will experience a sense of personal power and freedom unlike any you may have known.

Stop waiting for others to change, for things to get easier, or for you to feel like it. If you allow life's circumstances or the behavior of others to ruin your day, that's *your* choice. While you can't make others play fair, you *can* choose to be the kind of person you want to be, in each moment.

What kind of conversation are you? An odd question, perhaps, but from this perspective, your life is a conversation. You live through the lens of language. (A bit of poetic license here, but even getting up every morning is the result of a successful conversation—with yourself!) To see yourself as a conversation is a simple yet effective way to check in with your authenticity and your everyday reality. You *create* that reality by the kind of conversation you choose to be. The path involves learning to live with paradox, chaos, contradiction and mystery—appreciating everything from the wholeness of both. This is just what the fear-based mind wants to avoid, however, in its attempt to keep you safe. Lastly, the path means recognizing your opinions as "just ideas," voices in your head that you hold as "truth" largely because you're so used to having them as companions.

Personal Responsibility: A Practice of Authenticity. Replaying your thoughts, notice your *relationship* to each thought. Do you believe the thought? Is it uniquely your own? Were you aware of the thought at the time it occurred? Did you feel anxiety with your thoughts (clues they're not authentically your own)? Listen for "mismatches" among your intention, interpretation, emotion, listening or inner truth (authentic self) in all you say and do. Would others see me the way I see myself? Ask yourself if the overall patterns in your thinking would serve you well if you adopted them everywhere you go in life. Speak and listen from personal responsibility, not blame. With practice at this exercise, you'll notice a significant drop in volume, stress, intensity and fear in your conversations. *Advanced practice*: instead of taking responsibility only for what you **say**, could you take responsibility for how you're **heard**? Enroll others in your challenge; ask them to help by pointing out how they hear you, how *they* interpret *your* listening and speaking. If what they tell you makes you angry, you've lost the game. No judgment; just learning. New awareness creates change.

AN INVITATION

By adopting practices suggested here as everyday companions in your life, you'll be shifting your thinking to be far more inclusive and more aligned with your own personal truth. With felt experience of practice, your new thinking creates a true map to the territory of *your* life. You may even find, as I have, that the combination of conscious thought and a more inclusive context helps make decisions for you, thereby releasing you from the stress of life's little choices. What you will have done here is to exchange the outdated, unconscious "filter" of old assumptions and lessons for one created from your own truth, consciously chosen with deep clarity, as the context of your authentic self. The new filter renders most choices either so obvious you don't have to agonize over them, or so inconsequential they don't have to be made at all. The little stuff just no longer gets in the way of the big stuff.

To accept full responsibility for how your conversations go also means releasing the blame game 100%. No one else can "make you" do, say, or feel anything; nor can *they* be responsible for how *you* respond. **You** are. Your feelings belong to you, as do your interpretation, listening, intention and personal presence. Claiming responsibility for your communications' effectiveness may feel scary beforehand, yet it's curious how much freedom you feel once you do so. As always, practice creates the experience.

From a place of personal authenticity and self-trust, you realize you no longer need to have agendas, to control other people, to know outcomes ahead of time, to be backed into a corner by the bad behavior of others, or to censor your own presence. You just "show up," *being* your principles, and choosing your context. Then you allow the *natural feedback* within a conversation to show you the way, to the next step and the next. You just need to listen. Because you cannot possibly know or even anticipate every path a conversation can take, this self-trust and use of feedback offers all the freedom and skill you need.

Transformation is up to *you*. No one else in your life needs to change or help. True, you may still get cut off on the highway; your boss may still yell at you; your spouse may still get angry at old behaviors. What's different is *you*. When you *see* old things in new ways, you *respond* to old things in new ways. *Your* world will change when *you* change.

And now it's time to put this all to work—in a conversation.

HAVING THE CONVERSATION

Just as there are aspects of discovering, then reclaiming the *context* of your conversations, so, too, are there steps in framing the *content* of your conversations. These steps may seem awkward at first, but by applying conscious awareness and rigor early on, the result down the road is that your natural, effective self simply won't have to think so hard to make conversations constructive. They'll flow, simply because you do.

Probably no surprise by now, but even working on the *content* of your conversations has far more to do with awareness and thinking than with speaking. In fact, what you want to say will rarely be an issue if you ensure that the framework aligns with your emerging authentic self.

Let's begin a conversation. Whereas before, you might just "jump in" and start talking, now you see how crucial it is to prepare, both in your own mind and "on the table," before speaking your first word.

I suggest these "steps," taken one-at-a-time and with conscious awareness to start ... which will, with practice, flow into one. As you found in your self-reflective practice for elements of personal context, this offers you *felt experience* crucial to long-term change. Despite initial awkwardness, cementing the experience into your being will make a huge difference in your conversations, especially if and when a conversation involves conflict. The steps, with exploration to follow:

- In your mind, choose the kind of conversation you intend to have—is it to achieve a result, to explore new possibility, or just chat?

- In your mind, name the subject of your intended conversation.

- Draw your awareness to *your own* personal context in the moment—intention, interpretation, emotion, listening, and sense of true self.

- Draw your awareness to *the other's* personal context—"listening" best you can for what their consciousness is like in the moment.
- Speak (for the first time) with the other person, the first topic being the building of shared intention and context.
- Have the conversation.

Let's explore each of these in some detail. Given the prevalence of conflict in our world today, both personally and professionally, I've included a later section that deals only with conflict. First, let's look at things when they go well, as intended.

What kind of conversation are you having?

Conversations usually fall into one of three categories:

- ***Conversation for Action:*** the kind of conversation intended to produce results, action by one or both of you, to "get things done." A true conversation for action consists of a request (for action), a promise (to perform the action), and an agreement (what gets done, what "done" looks like when it's complete, and when).
- ***Conversation for Possibility:*** the kind of conversation intended to explore ideas, to generate future potential. This may *later* result in action, but for now, it's about new invention; no "conclusion." By freeing yourself to focus on what's possible, unconstrained by having to agree or create an action plan, you leverage creative genius.
- ***Conversation for Conversation:*** everything else. Getting to know someone, building rapport, having fun, idle chat, even complaint, drama, arguing and gossip. No result is intended or produced, although it may lead to something down the road.

None of these is better than another. Conversations for action might be more common and appropriate in the workplace, and you might find more "conversation for conversation" in a coffee shop, but each has its place. What matters is knowing which one you intend, or, if you've already started, which one you're having at the moment. If your manager wants you to take on a new project and you think it's hallway chatter, you'll probably miss the assignment. If your spouse wants to share her feelings and you think something needs to be fixed, you're probably headed for an argument.

If all you want is "conversation for conversation," you don't need much from this chapter. The rest of this chapter focuses on conversations for action and for possibility. Your discussion about the weather probably won't go poorly; nor will it prevent rain. But life often asks more of us than idle chat. With "conversations for possibility," and more so with "conversations for action," there's more preparation needed (know the context, have clear intention, be aware of interpretation, be emotionally intelligent, commit to active listening, read the energy in the room).

What's the intended subject of the conversation?

After choosing the kind of conversation you're having, it's time to name a subject—so you know what you plan to talk about. This serves to keep you focused, and to create shared space with the other person, space in which your conversation can "unfold" naturally. But the other significant value of naming a subject is so that, during the conversation, you can use your awareness to notice when the subject may stray from the intended one, and then bring things back, to *stay focused*. Here's why this matters.

Have you ever noticed how the topic of even a serious conversation can change, often many times over the course of a few minutes? This is a result of lack of clear awareness and intention on the part of the participants. Here are two examples; both show up as humorous, but they are far more representative than you may think.

- You've no doubt heard political interviews of some sort. What you may not have noticed is the outright disregard for subject on the part of the "official" being interviewed. *Interviewer*: Mr. Candidate, if elected, what will you do about environmental issues? *Candidate*: thank you for asking; let me tell you about my plans for economic stimulus. Almost *never* does the interviewer (or do listeners, apparently) notice the shift, for rarely is the "official" reminded he's not answering the question. For the interviewer, awareness of the subject, and an intention to stay on it would have changed this. For the candidate, personal integrity and transparency would have changed this. To me, *both* parties failed here.

- While I've shortened it to make the point, this kind of thing happens all the time, even in business meetings. I heard this one at Starbucks recently. *Jim*: It sure is chilly this morning. *Fred*: Oh, chili; my mom makes the best chili. *Jim*: Chile; have you ever been there; I hear it's beautiful. *Fred*: isn't that where Patagonia is? *Jim*: Oh, man, Patagonia; they make the best outdoor gear. ... You get the point. I've often kept track of the number of times subject changes in business meetings. More than once, I've counted 20 over such changes in 5 minutes. If these had been just "conversations for conversation," this would present no particular problem. But they were intended to get something done. There was almost no chance a result was achieved.

The subject of any conversation is a choice you make, and you don't make it just once, you make it in each moment. Without awareness, as you can see, the subject can change many times in a span of minutes. With awareness, you can guide any conversation in the direction you desire. As a practice, you might begin noticing both the intended subject of conversations as well as where and how the subject strays ... and if anyone notices. Start with conversations in which you are an observer; it's easier when you're not involved. Then move to those in which you are a participant.

What's the current state of your own personal context?

Once you've chosen a subject, and before starting a conversation, bring your awareness to your sense of self in that moment. This should be more natural now, after your regular practice of noticing elements of your context.

Check in with your *interpretation*, *emotional* frame and *listening*; by being aware of your "edges," you can better keep them neutral factors (ex: having feelings without becoming them). Think about the *intention* you have for the conversation—the kind of person you want to be, the personal principles you intend to express (to learn, connect, create, resolve, etc.; *vs.* to win, be right, control, judge). *Envision* the conversation going just how you intend; see yourself confidently being your true self. Envisioning creates a "memory of the future" so when you arrive, you "already know your way." As you gain self-trust, it's time to connect with another. After some practice at this, you'll be able to get a true and valid sense of yourself by checking in quickly with self-trust alone. You'll know easily; you'll feel it.

As self-trust grows, you may find that the "circumstances" surrounding your conversations seem less significant. That wonderful observation marks a huge shift—your well-being is now coming from your own truth, not someone else's opinion of you. That self-trust will now mark the *starting point* for your conversations. By the way, this is what distinguished the two conversations you recalled in the Introduction—in one, you were being yourself; in the other, you "couldn't."

How about the context of the other person?

By virtue of having practiced with your own contextual frame, you'll find you can sense the same in others. You'll be able to read intention, emotion, interpretation, listening, as well as overall personal responsibility in others. Trust your intuitive sense. You may feel you're making a guess. So be it. It will nevertheless be based in the quality of your growing ability to listen clearly and objectively, to both what's being said and what's not. Your "guess" becomes a beginning to check in with the other person.

I suggest, at first anyway, that you begin conversations with others by explicitly talking about context—naming the *subject* as you see it, asking for agreement; naming the *intention* you'd like for the conversation, asking for concurrence; declaring your own *context*—how you see yourself in the moment, with respect to interpretation, emotional state, concerns you may have, *responsibility* you intend to claim as your own.

If you're in doubt about theirs, ask them to do the same. Yes, this is awkward at first. But it cements your learning. It also makes a huge difference in the outcome of your communications. With both parties "on the same page," the stage is set for a constructive conversation before you even begin. Without that, you're taking your chances.

~~~

When aligned with yourself, speaking flows naturally; when aligned with others, conversations flow naturally.

~~~

And if, in this process, you discover you're *not* in shared agreement about the framework of the conversation, you have two choices: not have the conversation, or allow the *lack of agreement* to be the subject until you both figure it out. This kind of mismatch is always about the context, not the content, of the conversation. It has far less to do with what you want to say or how you want to say it, and more to do with the different ways you both may see and think; that's context. Seeing it for what it is allows you to work on the true issue, and not find yourself faced with contention or conflict halfway into a conversation. You get to this place by working on your thinking, alone and together. Contention disappears as context expands. You can do this in one of two ways:

- consciously expand *your* context (thinking) so you include what you know about *theirs*. This helps open possibility.

- *talk* about shared intention and approach. You can acknowledge that you both think differently, but you'd like to make the conversation work, perhaps by suspending judgments for a while. If you're aware of terms or topics you know don't match, you can talk about how you define the terms, to learn the thinking underneath. Often this involves being aware of your own triggers, too. To *not* do these things is to leave you vulnerable before you start. Note: agreeing on *context* is not the same as agreeing on *content*!

Despite all this, there will be those inevitable times when it's not clear how to resolve the mismatch, or times when it's clearly impossible to do so. Such conversations are likely headed for contention or conflict. The "winning strategy" here is to *know* that before you get into it! Following this process gives you that awareness. Awareness gives you choice. In the case that shared context is impossible, you now can say, "No, thank you," before a conversation even starts. More on this later, too.

Have the Conversation

An unconditionally constructive conversation is a **dialogue**—a *two-way* process of learning, with *mutually* satisfying outcomes, and conducted in an environment of *non-judgment*, acceptance of "what is," respect (whether you agree with them or not), safety and *trust* (for both yourself and the other person)— shared context. If you think a bit about each of the aspects of true dialogue, you realize how rare they are in our world today. Far more common, it seems, are one-way manipulations, monologues, and divisive exchanges that come more from opinion and judgment than from shared commitment to much of anything. Dialogue takes work ... *context* work.

Without belief in yourself, however, disagreements often devolve instead into *divisiveness*. Separation focuses on what's *wrong* instead of what's *possible*, and is driven by the need to protect rather than learn, valuing personal opinion and entitlement over resolution and mutual satisfaction. We see the impact of divisiveness very clearly in our world today. Fake news, alternative facts, hiding behind political correctness, all the yelling and drama that go along for the ride—signs of a system in breakdown, a system that has lost its way.

Experience has taught me that once a conversation begins, its flow is generally smooth, effective, respectful and shared when context homework has preceded it. That said, the most difficult part of any conversation, especially one you perceive as challenging, still remains how to begin. This has played out so consistently, both in my own life and in work with clients, that I rely on these two things alone—consciously-chosen context and an effective opening—confident that what follows will flow smoothly. I no longer need to plan or control the outcome of any conversation. So, how do you begin?

The best opening to any conversation is one that both *declares intention* and *broadens context* ... at the same time. This "instantly" creates a bigger space in which the conversation takes place, allowing you, and the other, more freedom to be authentic and more space for things to "flow." Here are a few entrées into common conversations that I've found meet both those criteria. Each of these is not only a conversation unto itself but is also a constructive starting point to more in-depth or complex conversations. Although each may appear trivially simple to you, ponder the impact each holds. It is surprising to me how *effective* some of these can be all on their own, yet, at the same time, how *rarely* they're used in any form whatsoever.

Effective conversation openings:

- The simplest conversation we rarely have: ***"Thank you."***
  (This opens space and softens tension.)

- The most powerful conversation we rarely have: *"I love you."* (Often a reminder, a way to set a big context simply.)

- The most freeing conversation we rarely have: *"No, thank you."* (This is an act of true *wisdom* for unresolvable conflict, and a way to eliminate the useless conversations that rob our time and spirit (which is most of them!))

- The highest potential conversation we rarely have: *"I need your help."* (This *invites* another *into* your context. Big.)

- The most courageous conversation we rarely have: *"I'm afraid."* (Being vulnerable is an act of courage, not the opposite; it invites connectedness.)

- A non-judgmental opening to an emotionally-charged conversation: *"Things just aren't working for me."* (This can be effective for performance reviews, personal disagreement, and even divorces.)

- A powerfully positive opening to any emotion or conflict-laden conversation: *"Help me understand."* (Again, invites the other into your context. This reduces tension, builds shared space.)

When you create a frame large enough to include your thinking **and** the thinking of the other person, a conversation becomes reciprocal and the potential for conflict falls away. Again, this does not guarantee that the other person will play, but it gives *you* space to use feedback from their response to guide your next steps, including saying, "no, thank you," and leaving. With your awareness, clarity, and sense of your own truth, this becomes easy.

Reflect on the suggested conversation openings above. What might they may have in common? A word that comes to my mind is *vulnerability*. A major barrier to effective communication, and a great contributor to contention and conflict, is the fear of being vulnerable. To say you don't know, to ask for help, to say you're afraid, even to say, "I love you," often evokes a fear response. Perhaps it's a fear of not knowing what comes next; perhaps it's a fear of being exposed; perhaps it's a fear of perceived loss of control; perhaps it's just the fear of being afraid. In her book *Daring Greatly*, Brené Brown offers what I think is the best perspective ever on vulnerability. To be vulnerable is an act of courage. Perhaps this is why discovering, becoming aware of, and managing your own personal context is so crucial. The self-trust you gain allows you to shift your seeing from fear/ vulnerability to trust/courage.

CONVERSATIONS INVOLVING CONFLICT

A common question at this point is: "my conversations are becoming easier and more effective, but how can it work when the topic or person (including me) feels contentious?" A 3-part answer, followed by some new perspective. Using ideas in this book, you can:

- avoid, or gracefully manage, most of the conflict you experience today, by anticipating it beforehand or resolving it smoothly when it occurs. You can do this on your own, independent of others.

- with a *willing* party, work to successfully resolve almost any conflict once it has started. The other party doesn't need to have exposure to all you've learned, just a willingness to work together.

- with an *unwilling* party, know when to *decline* or *leave* a contentious conversation. You cannot *make* someone cooperate; wisdom is knowing when, and how, to decline or leave a conversation.

The *potential* for conflict is an inherent part of both life and language. But potential need not become reality. Most contention originates *not* from life's situations but from an *interpretation*, even if unconscious, one that goes something like this: I'm not willing to accept *current* reality as reality, and am therefore determined to turn it into a *different* reality. In other words, I don't like the *way things really are*, so I'm going to make things the *way they should be*. Notice the underlying assumption: things *should* be a certain way. Situations don't cause conflict; *the way we think* about them does. We have conflict in our lives because we *choose* it. And we need not choose it intentionally; it happens by default when we're unaware of the thoughts that keep it alive.

If, like most, you learned a lot of assumptions and rules early in life, then you tend to see more of life's experiences as threats or problems—so you unconsciously defend "the way life is supposed to be."

If, on the other hand, you learned that you create your experience of reality through the power of your thinking, then you tend to see life's events more as an opportunity to learn and grow than as a series of problems. In this sense, a *problem* is what's left over when you're no longer willing to learn. Same situations; different responses.

As with any aspect of communication, coming to see and think about it in a new way helps to create new possibility. With contention, a "new way" to see it is that we choose contention, unconsciously of course, by making the judgments we make about ourselves, others, and the world.

Here are some key points about resolving conflict, many of which run counter to "prevailing wisdom."

- Conflict is less about "the issue" and more about your *thinking* about the issue.
- It's not about winning, or even about truth; it's about resolution.
- It's not about changing the other person; it's about choosing a path that offers peace ... for you.
- It's not about changing the situation, either; "the way it is" is the only thing you can count on.

- It's not about having defense or fighting skills, but about awareness and self-trust.

- The enemy is never a human being (unless it's yourself).

- Resolution is about respect, empathy, compassion, acceptance, understanding, values, patience and communication.

- Acceptance does not mean agreement; nor does it mean giving in, or staying resentful.

- Resolution entails preserving your own personal power vs. giving it away, so that you come out of the conversation "whole."

Just think: if you didn't believe you had to get your way, change others, have life "turn out," defend yourself, etc., it would mark the end of most blame, conflict and strife. As you learn to deal with yourself, others, and life "as they are," not "as you think they should be," you begin to release the *thinking* that drives conflict. Let go of the idea that something or someone has to be "wrong" and the majority of conflict would simply disappear. This is a classic example of the *interpretation* at work.

Outdated lessons have left us believing there are two ways to greet conflict ... deny it, burying it inside us—a strategy of *silence*; or control it—a strategy of *violence*. To choose either, however, comes from thinking there's a need to defend yourself. How about this instead: when you start to feel furious, it's time to get curious.

Did you ever stop to ask where that thinking came from, and perhaps consider another way? Despite wishes, life doesn't change for us until we *do* consider another way. But here's the problem. If you're in the midst of defending yourself, you're not going to stop and search for a better way. If you're *not* in the midst of defending yourself, you don't need to! So the question often goes unconsidered. What if now could be the time to step back and take a fresh look at what's happening?

By choosing to look *consciously* at the thinking that underlies your behavior, you come to see yourself and others more clearly, more objectively. Just by *noticing* your thoughts, (as most of the suggested practices up until now have promised), you open yourself to asking new questions. What if it simply didn't matter what anyone said? What if their words were simply a reflection of what's true *for them* and had nothing to do with me? What if I didn't feel the need to defend myself; what's possible then?

The natural state of the *conscious* human mind is calm curiosity and wonder. It wants to *understand*. It wants to learn. Learning doesn't require a response. Understanding is non-judgmental. Understanding is not the same as agreeing. Learning is an opening to collaboration. And that's where better relationships begin. Understanding self leads to understanding others. This is not about continually tolerating bad behavior from others, but about evoking the non-judgmental personal clarity inside you, clarity that releases the need to engage.

For these reasons, you approach conflict effectively by stepping beyond the need to make someone "wrong," beyond the place where someone or something "should be" a certain way. This means *shifting your level of consciousness*, not stifling your feelings, learning new skills, or controlling others. That place is a "high ground," a place above the contention inherent in a position-based, win-lose stance. If conflict or the potential for it became an opportunity for *learning*, (about yourself, others, life, etc.), you might approach such situations with curiosity, rather than anger or fear. From the high ground, you focus your awareness on seeing *what is*—without judgment. This means releasing interpretation.

All this means that the true enemy in conflict is rarely another person or even the "truth," but a way of thinking. When you become a relentless student of how you (and others) see and think, you can choose always choose a high-ground path. Only two ways of being will take you to new possibility, whether in everyday life or in conflict: *respect for others* and *trust in self.* This reciprocity leads naturally to dialogue.

Two quotes I love about conflict: (authors unknown):

- you don't have to attend every argument you're invited to
- never waste your time trying to explain who you are to people who are committed to misunderstanding you.

INVITATION AND CHALLENGE

Constructive conversations are authentic conversations. And you make your *conversations* authentic by making *yourself* authentic. And you do that, not by knowing more or trying harder, but by becoming so aware of your own thinking (your personal context) that you are 100% free to choose each thought, in each moment. No longer will those old beliefs and lessons cloud your vision, preventing the authentic you from being itself. You enter the world of self-trust.

I've taken it on as a personal challenge to make every conversation I have a constructive one, no matter the topic, the emotion, the stakes, the other person, or even the fact that I'm an introvert. To do this, I found it helpful at first to say, "no, thank you" to many conversations I deem as unlikely to be fruitful. As awareness of my own thinking grew, I was able to release one old "story" after another. With each story from the past that I let go, along with it I found I could let go of saying "no, thank you" to one more dubious conversation. Self-trust was growing. I am now at the point where I reserve "no, thank you" only for the most intransigent of the opinionated others that seem so prevalent today in our world. For the majority, however, it has become more of a game to me; in what ways can I contribute to a constructive conversation?

In closing, I invite the same for you. Make it a big personal experiment. You might start by telling yourself that the only way you fail is that you choose to not learn from whatever happens as you take on the ideas and practices suggested here. You even have a "free pass" for conversations that feel difficult at first: "No, thank you." As you learn more about your thinking, the number of free passes you claim (from yourself) will drop dramatically. As self-trust grows, you may even find some humor in the idea that you've replaced "no, thank you" with "bring it on." You need never again give your power away to someone else. Nor need you ever exert power over someone else. It simply won't cross your mind.

Lastly, I'm often asked about applying this material to everyday situations at work. Many workplaces are "nurseries for contention," driven as they commonly are by position power, false authority, lack of clarity, and emotional imbalance. I'll close with sharing the notes from a workshop I did with a management team in a medium-sized company. They were committed to improved communication amongst themselves, yet didn't know how. After a few hours of "constructive conversation," this is what they came up with—a new agreement for their workplace. I honor their dedication and intention. May others follow suit.

IDEAS FOR THRIVING WORKPLACES

- *"That was then; this is now."* Release conversation about the past. Even if it was 10 seconds ago, the only thing I can change now is what I do next. Ask *"What's possible?"* not *"Who's to blame?"*

- *"It is what it is."* No matter the situation or the circumstances that created it, it is what *it* is. Possibility and personal power come from *what I do next.* If I choose complaint, I'm giving my power away.

- *"If I use yesterday to predict what may happen tomorrow, then tomorrow will probably turn out alarmingly similar to yesterday."* Prediction can't create a positive future; invention does. I am its inventor. Why invent yesterday when I can invent tomorrow?

IDEAS FOR HEALTHY
CONVERSATIONS AT WORK

It's up to us, individually and as a team, to agree to *follow* these at work (*and* outside work if we choose), and to *support* each other in upholding them. So while we all may *have* fears, we still *choose* our behaviors:

- I won't use email for communication with emotional or personal impact. Face-to-face only for such topics.

- Accepting a group or management decision means committing to it. If I disagree, so be it. To "*disagree with attitude*" is not acceptance.

- I will not come to conclusions before asking questions.

- For any issues or problems, I will go directly to the person involved first, and have a personal conversation with them, with compassion.

- After working with the individual directly, I no longer need to waste energy talking behind anyone's back; so I won't. This is an act of *personal integrity* for me, and an act of *mutual respect* for us both.

- I will not raise my voice in the workplace. It's OK to "feel angry" but it's not OK to lash out in anger. They are different.

- I will process "issues" and "mistakes" collaboratively, with compassion for others.

- I will choose an attitude that matches the workplace in which I want to work, knowing that attitude **creates** the workplace in which I work. Attitude is always a **choice**!

- I will help others stay empowered to make these agreements part of the way all of us live and work.

Chapter 5

Authentic Connection

In Nature's Image

"The first peace is that which comes within the souls of people when they realize their relationship, their oneness, with the universe and all its powers, and when they realize that at the center of the universe dwells Wakan-Taka (the Great Spirit), and that this center is really everywhere, it is within each of us."

– Black Elk, Oglala Sioux

INTRODUCTION

Imagine for a moment that you could live creatively and sustainably, with both resilience and balance, regardless of circumstances. You can.

Imagine for a moment that you could view life's chaos and challenges not as issues but as invitations to your creative genius. You can.

Imagine for a moment that you could experience life with calm and creative confidence, and at the same time be wildly productive. You can.

To me, this is what it means to lead a truly vibrant human life—deeply connected to self and world; fully expressing your unique, creative essence; experiencing the peace, freedom and joy that result from enriching your internal world while being a contribution to the external world.

Living **"In Nature's Image"** opens the possibility for you to live with greater freedom, resilience, peace, meaning and authenticity—by listening to, then honoring, the simple yet elegant lessons offered by nature. Viewing your life through the lens of nature's principles is one of many ways to approach "living authentically." As with other approaches, this one assumes you have completed Part I of the Living Authentically program beforehand. (Chapters 1, 2 and 3)

With an *external* world marked by chaos, complexity, uncertainty and paradox, it's my view that we have lost sight of what truly matters, a deeper reality guiding our *internal* world. By accepting a promise that we can find happiness adopting the thinking of *others*, we've thereby denied ourselves a connection with both our uniqueness (that innate, creative essence that makes you *you* ... or *soul*) and our oneness (the connectedness we share with all life ... or *spirit*). Unaware of this, however, we miss the fact that in relying on the external world we've lost touch with our inner truth, and with it, our greatest potential.

So while we may have come to see things like social media, cell phones and shopping as signs of being alive, they're more likely signs of being numbed and distracted by life. Lost, we blame *life*. I believe we have misidentified the enemy. **Life** is not the problem. **How we see and think** about life is what has left us in the quiet desperation of our own unconscious, life-limiting thinking.

I liken this situation to following a roadmap that has no resemblance whatsoever to the landscape in which we travel. Through unconscious and rigid adherence to that map, however, we've become lost, with neither our awareness nor consent. Because this map is the only one we know, we don't have the tools to find our way home.

We need a new map, one that depicts the true territory of our lives. That map, I suggest, is right in our backyards—*the way it is* in nature. The same principles that have guided life here on Earth for over four billion years offer us a ready-made and accessible map back to the possibility we long for, a path home to who we've always been.

This chapter is neither a nature study guide nor a science book. It does not ask you to love (or understand) nature or her processes. It doesn't even offer truly new ideas, for all of life has followed this same set of principles for eons. Rather, it offers *new* perspectives on *old* ideas—the simple thought that, as creatures of nature, we might reconnect with the inner truth of our original source, and rekindle those same principles in the way we see, think, speak and behave about the potential our lives hold. I also offer my personal viewpoint, based on years of experience and challenge in navigating the territory of my own life; and, over the past 20 years, helping hundreds of others to navigate theirs. So, their stories, my stories, and my love for nature offer the fuel for this chapter. My intention is that together they may open you to seeing your journey in a way that serves you *and* the world more fully and authentically.

I invite you to join me in a conversation that has become my life, an exploration into how we believe, see and think ... and how that has influenced the way we speak, relate and behave ... which in turn creates the reality we now experience. Through my life experience, I've found that by truly understanding how and why we think the way we do, we create powerful openings for change. By coming to accept and embrace "the way we *think* it is" today, with both clarity and non-judgment, we can step confidently and naturally into "the way it *could* be" tomorrow.

In chapters ahead, you'll see how living in nature's image leads you into your deepest truth and potential. In the process, you'll come to:

- See why society's prevailing life model does not, and cannot, work, yet see how you've been lured into adopting and living it as valid

- See how living more in tune with nature's principles can help you tap your innate potential more powerfully than you may have imagined

- Create a new vision, or map, to the territory of your future, one that puts you squarely in the center of an infinite, benevolent universe

- See nature's way in a new light, one that makes her principles both accessible and relevant to today's living, a model for your own life—without "doing science" or hugging trees, (unless you want to!)

Let's set out for the territory and see what it has to teach.

An Overview of Personal Practice

The practices suggested here as ways to incorporate each of nature's principles into your everyday life build upon the foundation practices you've already adopted—(1) a practice of silence, and (2) a practice of observing your thinking. The benefit to this approach is that, as you add an exercise for each principle to your daily practice, you'll be building a single, integrated practice of self-awareness that offers all you need so your authentic self emerges (or better said, re-emerges), naturally.

As a recap, here's a summary of those two basic practices:

Personal silence: Perhaps no more powerful in the journey to transformation, yet no more misunderstood, is a practice of personal silence. A regular practice of calming the mind is a pathway to your deepest truth and greatest potential. Sit quietly alone for 20 to 30 minutes each day. Relax your body, take a few deep breaths. Focus on a simple object in your view. Breathe purposefully; just listen. Be present; there's no right or wrong. You'll likely find thoughts continually arising, often in the form of inner voices (things to do, fears, etc.) View them as passing clouds; just watch each as it goes by. Silence focuses your awareness on the present moment. That's the moment you tend to *miss* while you're using your energy to worry about the *next* moment instead.

Observe your thoughts: If you're not aware of your thinking, life is driven by an incessant flow of unconscious voices you *think* is thinking. Only by interrupting this flow will you know your truth. As an *observer* of your thoughts, you gain a perspective on your consciousness you'd never get as a *participant* alone. When you see your thoughts at work, you can trace them back to the old assumptions, beliefs and lessons that created them. This allows you to make new choices for your "beliefs." *Stop* what you're doing three or four times a day. During a few moments of quiet reflection, replay in your mind thoughts you've had since the last replay, as if a movie with you as its audience. *Listen* to what they tell you. Resist judging or trying to change them. Just notice.

Each practice suggested in the pages ahead asks you to set aside 15 - 20 minutes of dedicated personal time each day. Each follows the format of the basic practices above and is designed to enhance self-discovery by exposing ways in which you can connect your everyday longing with nature—naturally. With practice, you become deeply aware of your consciousness, and in the process, *become* "nature's way." You will find it helpful to journal what you discover about yourself.

THE WAY IT ALWAYS WAS ... STILL IS

"We make our world significant by the courage of our questions and by the depth of our answers."
– Carl Sagan

My view of how life works differs significantly from the lessons I was taught as a child—the ones about life's mechanistic, linear, cause-and-effect nature, and about the rational-only nature of my own personal presence. By contrast, experience has taught me that life flows effortlessly if modeled on nature's ways. (Life works the way **nature** works, not the way *classical* **science** *says* it works.) Today, nature's wisdom frames my seeing and thinking, and in turn, life and work. It forms the invisible backdrop for my coaching. Each of nature's principles has held up in the face of every challenge, crisis or question I've encountered, with myself or with others. In that sense, I'm comforted by the unity they offer. It's not about becoming a scientist or a nature lover, or even understanding each point. It's about embracing the holistic perspective they embody. Therein lies the opening to our dream of a thriving future.

Because I've come to trust nature's way as a coherent, sustainable model of how my life works best, I now find, when challenges present themselves, I'm continually drawn to the same question: "What would nature do here?" From early childhood adventures, to deep connection with nature as an adult, to 20 years leading nature tours in North America's majestic wilderness settings, to simple daily walks in the woods, I experience nature as compassionate listener to my pressing questions and as quiet teacher for life's (and my own) mysteries. Through the consistent answers offered over many years, coupled with purposeful practice to allow nature's ways to teach me, I now rely on them automatically.

With persistence, non-judgment and consistency, nature has taught me:

- to CREATE, with *intention*. What do I hear when I listen to my inner voice? How might I honor the deep personal truth to which I'm drawn? Is my life an expression of what matters most to me?

- to LIVE, with *awareness*. Possibility shows up in "the space between," in emptiness. Opportunity depends on change. What is my relationship to silence? to change? to not knowing?

- to ACT, with *courage*. Rarely can outcomes be known ahead of time. Can I trust the power of my own truth to guide my path in life? How does faith light my way?

- to RELATE, with *reverence,* to myself and to others. How I think, speak and act profoundly affects my life, and the lives of others. Do I live with deep gratitude for all I've been given?

Curiously, whenever I feel drawn to this kind of consistency over and over, I want to explore even *more* deeply—to find the universal truths beneath the surface. What life forces drive the universe? How are they expressed on Earth? How can I learn about myself from the way nature sustains life? How might I "re-member" (put back together) those lost parts of me, as a way to reconnect with the ultimate source of life?

So I look back to a time that predated our modern ways, so as to understand what life may have been like then, and what ideas or truths may have framed the existence of early cultures. This exercise is not about discarding the advances we've made as a species, but about discovering the oneness that no doubt characterized life in a simpler time, a time when connectedness and community ran much deeper than they seem to do today, unfettered by today's complexity.

Our planet's original cultures lived in reverence and reciprocity with nature, within a framework, or context, that viewed everything—energy, matter, consciousness, spirit, indeed all of life, animate and inanimate—as one. They learned to listen to their world; what they heard taught them all they needed to know. Although their ways came before modern knowing, they "knew without knowing," intuitively, deeply.

From the depth and oneness of original cultures to the strained divisiveness of today's society, the way it always was ... still is, although now hidden under outdated beliefs that have caused us to trade away that deepest part of self, and led us far astray from the natural harmony of life our predecessors once knew. What might they teach us today, could they speak to the dilemma in which we find ourselves?

Here's my take on life's universal truths, truths early people no doubt lived. Although I'm not here to "do science" or to prove nature's laws, this is my perspective on how adopting nature's way has helped me reclaim what I long for—a deep connection with my inner truth, my connection to all of life, and life's natural flow as well.

- the universe is defined by remarkable, natural order: "all is one"

- how nature works is the expression of that order here on Earth; it's just below the surface chaos we know as life

- we are part of that order; only unconsciously held assumptions and beliefs give us an illusion of separateness, when in fact, none exists

- *life* isn't the problem we believe it to be; the way we *see* life has left us lost ... from following a map that exists only in our minds

- we're constrained by a map of the *past*, not the *future*, a map designed to protect us from our *limitations*, not inspire our *potential*

- the map's periphery is our *worldview*, rooted in classical science, that sees life as mechanistic, linear and without inherent meaning

- science is not *the world*, but a process to help *understand* the world

- life doesn't work how *science* works; it works how *nature* works

- each of us is an ecosystem; *thinking* is the energy fueling our ecosystem; life-limiting thinking inhibits its sustainability

- we need a worldview/map that accurately describes the territory of our lives, encompassing the rich breadth and depth of subjective human experience

- our map is personal, created *consciously and individually*, based on what's true *for us.* This demands commitment and awareness

- life is practice; we *become* what we *practice.* If we are to become our authentic truth, we must live the practice of that truth, getting to *know* the territory of our ways of seeing, thinking and speaking

Based in this learning, here is a summary of eight principles that portray what I've learned and experienced from "nature as teacher," principles that have become my life context, and have helped me know my place in the universe. The next pages explore these principles in more detail.

- **Creative Expression**: The purpose of life is not a result, but a *process*—of creative expression. It's a process that spawns amazing productivity with neither control nor agenda

- **Opportunism**: Life is *opportunistic*, filling openings in time and space. Uncertainty and chaos invite creativity

- **Self-organization**: Life creates order from chaos, naturally, by listening to *feedback*, information inherent in every living system

- **Simultaneity:** There's no independent reality; truth depends on context; all possibilities always exist, simultaneously
- **Rhythm:** Life's recurring patterns, not the events comprising them, are the carriers of meaning; patterns renew and refresh
- **Energy:** Energy is a measure of creative expression; none is wasted
- **Community:** Sustainability favors cooperation through relationships
- **Connectedness:** All life is one; everything is interconnected

PRINCIPLE #1: CREATIVE EXPRESSION

"Nature does not hurry, yet everything is accomplished."
– Lao Tzu

Summary: The entire universe is sustained by a singular energy— the *process of creative expression*, each element expressing its innate essence. This suggests that life isn't a *destination* or result to be attained, but rather a *journey* to be experienced. The creative process is the wellspring from which all possibility unfolds, energy that drives meaningful lives and thriving workplaces. *What if you could design your entire life around that deep personal truth to which you are continually drawn?*

Nature's Principle: To create is to bring into existence, to transform "what isn't" into "what is"—building bridges between possibility and reality. Our vast universe is sustained by a singular energy, the energy of creative expression. This idea introduces the first principle of life, creative process as purpose. From the instant of the Big Bang some 14 billion years ago, the universe has been *always becoming*. Never has anything been static, nor will it ever be. Things are always being created, whether stars, galaxies, trees, canyons, snowflakes or humans. Things are always passing, whether stars, galaxies, trees, canyons, snowflakes or humans. The products of creation come and go, yet the process that creates them is sustained. The universe is a process—of creation and re-creation.

Nature also tells us that each thing, animate or inanimate, creates according to its own unique essence. Essence is that part of a thing it can't *not* be. A maple tree springs from a tiny seed, then branches toward the sky. Stars coalesce out of dust and gas in space and burn for eons from the accumulated mass and pressure. A polar bear has embedded in its DNA all it needs to be the ultimate Arctic marine hunter. Nothing *but* a polar bear could express itself in this unique way. Maple seeds can't grow up to become polar bears. Polar bears can't decide to go to college so as to get a better job. Each is uniquely suited for its own essence. Creative expression drives the universe. Stars, trees and bears come and go; the process that creates them goes on.

The Opening Offered: As creatures of nature, we humans are also here for the purpose of creative expression. Creativity isn't just *part* of who we are; it's the *essence* of who we are. Often, we refer to as *soul*, or essence, that specific part of each of us that's unique, an individual creative energy so deep and strong that it drives our lives, whether we consciously believe it, see it, honor it … or not. It's the energy that pulls at us throughout life. When we come to know and honor it consciously, we can align our lives with this, our authentic truth. For a window into essence, observe a young child; we see wonder, curiosity, creativity. Expressing those traits throughout life is how we learn and grow; it's who we're meant to be. The source of meaning is in the creativity that fuels soul journeys. Sadly, this uniqueness is often squeezed aside as we grow up, a price we pay to learn the "ways of the world." What we "knew without knowing" as children, we now must re-learn as adults.

Prevailing Wisdom: If these ideas sound strange, it's because we've been taught to see them as such. We've learned that if we're being creative, we're not "working." Because we've also learned that hard work is key to our success, we come to deny our creative spirit, our deepest essence, and with that, the source of the true meaning and happiness we long for in our lives. We've been lured away from our belief in authentic truth by a false promise of something bigger from the external world.

The Opportunity/Promise: What if life were about the experience of our creative essence, not about results or destination? What if we're here as human "beings," not "doings?" When we regain our connection with our essence, we'll discover that creative expression is not just *a* force, but the *driving* force, in a life of meaning and purpose—and results! When we become co-creators in this process of always becoming, we can use our uniqueness to illuminate the path ahead, experiencing the depth and meaning life has to offer. In designing our lives around the messages of our own inner truth, we can open up possibilities we'd never even have envisioned while we were out there trying to control things. This is not about giving up on achievement. It's about seeing that we can achieve more by *being* more, not trying so hard *doing* more.

Nature's Story: The Grand Canyon: a mile deep, up to 15 miles wide, almost 300 miles long. A plaster cast of it would make an impressive mountain range. It has taken the Colorado River about 5 million years to carve the canyon we see today. The river is old, yet it's a child compared to the 2 *billion*-year-old rocks it bisects. The Grand Canyon offers lessons in patience, uncertainty, acceptance, and of course, process rather than outcome. While we "strut and fret our hour upon the stage," nature is quietly doing what she has done for eons. No plan, no agenda, no goal; just a focus on process, the essence; in this case, a river being a river. There was never a plan to create the Grand Canyon. There still isn't. The canyon isn't even an *outcome*. It's just the current state of the continual *process* of creation. "River" is a verb. There is no struggle to achieve. The river isn't *trying* to wear down the rocks; rocks don't fight back. Nature *holds* water without holding *onto* water. Water changes the shape of all it touches yet competes with nothing.

My Story: For 40 years of adult life, I unconsciously lived society's "prevailing wisdom." I placed a premium on the idea that by knowing more, trying harder and staying busy, I'd make money and achieve happiness. It didn't work. I made money, yet I had been doing life, not being Brad. When the stress caught up with me, I realized there was more to life, and to me. I'd lost two marriages and missed a lot of my two sons' childhoods. I began to see in a new way. For the first time, I began looking inside, where I found real answers, instead of outside, where I'd been taught to look. Through the practices offered here, I discovered that my life had always been offering clues to my true essence, but I'd been unaware of their messages. The way I've now come to know my essence is this: *I help enhance perspective and clarity so as to evoke new possibility.* In tracing my life experiences as far back as I could, I found I was always pulled to drawing bigger frames around a subject so as to find deeper truth, awareness, or possibility. I even recalled my parents saying my sixth-grade math teacher had to go home and study at night because she was afraid of questions I might ask.

Despite my innate love for math and the sciences, I recall the dichotomy of education's preoccupation with "using formulas" over a deeper and richer way of knowing and learning. As a manager in the software world, I avoided software, business and computers, focusing instead on reframing our work so managers on my team could do a better job. At age 50, I realized this was the essence of coaching, helping others reframe their lives so more is possible. I became a coach, to help others live lives they love. This is a coaching book; I'm here to help you reframe how you see and think so more is possible for you, too.

Even though it took me until age 50 to discover this inner truth, it has become an amazing, as well as unexpected, source of both clarity and freedom for me. *Clarity* because I run every choice and every thought through the filter of that one truth—how it fits with the unity of all I "know." If it passes, I know it's right; if it fails, I don't do it. *Freedom* because knowing what matters allows me to commit to that, fully aware that it will serve me in a meaningful way. I am grateful for the process.

An Invitation: What do you care about so deeply that you'd devote your life to its fulfillment? What if you could see just a bit further or bigger than today; what possibility might you find just beyond the edge of your current perception? What if mistakes are about learning, not about being wrong? What if you didn't have to have so much, want so much, need so much, or achieve so much, and could allow yourself to simply *be* more?

Practice: *Discovering your own personal truth.* Until you know what matters most to you, your energy is *unconsciously* devoted to upholding outdated beliefs about how life "should be," (which you eventually discover is what matters least!) Your innate creative essence has always been part of you. It's who you *really* are, and it wants to express itself through how you live—your soul's purpose, life mission, your unique truth. You feel its energy many times a day, pointing to your truth, asking you to listen. You discover it by *noticing*! This practice is a life-long inquiry into what matters to you. It creates a beacon illuminating your life's path. Later practices offer help in learning to trust, and follow, the light of your inner truth; this one is aimed at discovering it and making it your own. Every day—and it may take weeks, even months, of doing this to gain the depth and clarity needed to sustain it—sit quietly; absorb the *you* you've come to know. Instead of taking a linear view of life, from childhood forward, review *aspects* of your life. Possibilities include education, family, transitions, jobs, hobbies, relationships. Overlap is OK. Now, as a replay, look *inside each aspect*, one at a time, separate from the others, asking yourself: Who was I always being? What was I always drawn to? What did I wonder or imagine? What did I do whether I gained approval or not? Look for places in your "always" stories that ran against convention. One of mine from school: "I don't care about formulas; tell me how it works and I'll give *you* the formula." Not popular, but it was me. After considering each aspect of your life this way, review notes and find what's *common* in your lists. As you discover who you can't *not* be/do, you're guided to that piece of yourself that is so naturally you that you may have missed your unique essence (soul, purpose). Absorb the energy of this!

PRINCIPLE #2: OPPORTUNISM

"We all continually move on the edges of eternity, and are sometimes granted vistas through the fabric of illusion."
– Ansel Adams

Summary: Against a backdrop of continual change, life seizes the uncertainty of each moment, propagating itself in all directions, the essence of creative spirit. We therefore create our path in life by walking it, not by having it laid out ahead of time. Our most powerful tools, then, are *patience*, to wait for openings; *awareness*, to notice when they occur; *acceptance*, that life will unfold so as to serve us; and *trust*, in our own innate essence. *What if you could view life's inherent uncertainty as an opportunity for your creative genius rather than as a threat to your safety?*

Nature's Principle: In the view of classical science, a system responds smoothly to change; it's said to be linear. A change in one thing causes change in other things. Life, however, is non-linear. Life is uncertain; openings to possibility happen in response to always-changing conditions. Nature steps into the open space provided with her creative process, spreading life as she goes. Nature doesn't have to *try* to do this. Remaining open to opportunity, which actually comes from *not* trying, she *allows* the process to do the work. This is how the universe coalesced into galaxies, stars and planets. It's how evolution continues to mold life in the midst of change and uncertainty. Shifts in resources create openings; nature's process steps in, creating in three different ways: *replication*—making more of the same in easy times; *improvement*—making what already exists better during stressful times; *innovation*—creating something new, beyond earlier conception, in times of chaos. "Quantum change" arises when small openings result in big leaps, vastly different from creating according to a step-wise plan. With these first two principles together, creativity and opportunism, we can now say the following: life's inherent uncertainty and unpredictability create *opportunity*; *creative expression* flourishes by filling the void offered. Without uncertainty, there'd be no room for opportunity, and therefore no place for creativity to happen.

The Opening Offered: True throughout the universe, creativity is a natural state. It's *our* natural state too, although we've "forgotten" this, having allowed life's inherent complexity, uncertainty and chaos to block us. How we live has become *dependent on life's circumstances*, not on our own power of creative genius. In believing we need to control life, we actually inhibit the very opportunity we want most, because opportunity shows up when conditions permit, not just when we *want* it. Nature's way says we'd be far less stressed and more productive if we *allowed* things to happen instead. In this world, we no longer need "command and control" skills, but rather: *patience*, to wait for change; *awareness*, to notice change when it occurs; *acceptance*, that life will unfold in a way that will serve us; and *trust*, in our own power of creative expression. It's an adaptive strategy with big returns. However, it flies in the face of what we've been taught about the need for safety in our lives. Perhaps we need to redefine *safety* as well. Safety isn't about knowing we have it all handled, but knowing we have *what it takes* to handle it all. Life's uncertainty is not a threat, but an opening for blossoming of the natural creative genius inside us. Nothing new happens without opportunity; opportunity exists only because of uncertainty.

Prevailing Wisdom: We've been taught to be busy, work hard, achieve results, and make life happen via control. If our choice to live that way makes us the only creatures to experience dissatisfaction and stress, however, we might want to take a second look at our rules. The idea of relying on innate creative potential rather than on force is a huge shift for most of us to contemplate. It would strike most as a waste of time to be patient until conditions are right. More often than not, we believe that if we're to have opportunities in life, it's because we force them into being. In fact, we're powerless to exert this kind of control over our lives. Our power lies in a new way of seeing instead, learning to see uncertainty as a *possibility* instead of a *threat*.

The Opportunity/Promise: How can we learn to step into our own natural creative essence? A first step is to embrace uncertainty. Uncertainty pushes us to the edges of our comfort zones, yet we guard our comfort zones with vigilance—to keep us comfortable! Our response to reaching one of our edges is so automatic we rarely notice ourselves doing it—we retreat to the perceived safety of the center of our comfort zone. If we stopped and *examined* the edge instead, it would be easy to take the first step beyond it. In so doing, we'd tap our innate creative genius and experience a sense of freedom, too. Free to choose not only the steps we take but the attitude with which we approach life, our world gets much bigger very quickly. We can make our world as large and open as we like, or so small and difficult that little is possible. Our worldview, or context, determines how we'll respond to life's opportunities. If worldview says that little is possible, opportunities will pass us by; we simply fail to notice them. If we *see* possibility everywhere, it materializes everywhere. Consciousness makes all the difference.

Nature's Story: About 100,000 years ago, an instant in evolutionary time, some brown bears living on North America's Arctic coasts started to hunt from the edges of the sea instead of from land and rivers alone. Those who succeeded in catching seals from the winter ice extended their range north. With change in behavior and habitat came change in biology. Some of nature's change is cataclysmic, yet most happens slowly compared to our ability to see. Bears most adept at Arctic marine hunting were those with lighter fur, a great adaptation in an all-white environment. Those with longer snouts were better able to snag seals from holes in the ice. Those with sticky footpads and shorter ears were better able to negotiate ice and extreme cold. Many generations of "stepping into opportunity" gave birth to the polar bear. Science names two processes at work: adaptation to environment and natural selection. Today's polar bear is the ultimate Arctic carnivore, so well adapted to life in this hostile environment that the only heat that shows up on an infrared photograph is its breath! Nothing inside a brown bear offered evidence of the emergence of polar bears. The niche of "ultimate Arctic marine carnivore" was empty, inviting opportunity. Although nature doesn't envision specific possibility, she's always poised to step into an uncertain future with invention. Nature tries stuff out and keeps what works.

My Story: In the 1980s, I managed Digital Equipment Corporation's software publishing business. I'd been an engineer and engineering manager for 20 years, and by most accounts, including mine, I was the worst plant manager they ever had. I recall going to my manager to admit my shortcomings and ask for help. He offered the help I needed; I was grateful. His most amazing gift was a comment as I left his office. "You need to remember you're the only one who has ever managed that business who actually *knows* what's inside those $%^&* boxes." It took me a few days, but the impact of his words dawned on me. Perhaps he *didn't* know the impact; maybe I always *did* know. The value of software is not in the media on which it resided (then), but in the *information*; all my engineering experience until then had been with "information as value"—intellectual property. I felt free. Opportunity greeted me when I least expected it, and perhaps most needed it. I began to redefine the business as an information business, not a "boxes" business. (As I write this today, I realize how our world has changed in 30 years. Software, *in boxes*? A *question* that intellectual property has value?) At a deeper level, the opportunity offered even more. My ways of seeing and thinking had been freed as well, invited to explore outside the box, literally and figuratively. Perhaps "they" knew the potential of having an engineer manage an operations business; it took me a bit longer to notice. I was stuck "inside the box."

These same ideas continue to impact my life today; encouraging me to seek, then step beyond, edges of my current perception or comfort zone. I no longer miss so much, because I know I'm part of a bigger world.

An Invitation: How would life change if you viewed uncertainty as an opportunity to be approached with curiosity and creativity rather than as a threat to be approached with fear or control? What's your relationship to empty space? To silence? Is silence an irritant, or a source of curiosity, respect and reverence, for life and for yourself? Do you trust life enough to allow the open space and uncertainty to teach you? Seizing opportunity in each *uncertain* moment is the essence of creative spirit.

Practice: *Observing spaces between:* Opportunities exist everywhere. Only your level of awareness dictates whether you notice, or act. If life is full, there's no room for the new. Opportunity often lurks in the quiet spaces, spaces you miss while you're busy with life. Despite attempts to know the unknowable, predict the unpredictable, and convert chaos to order, you truly don't know what's next, and you simply can't control it. And to be honest, don't you think that if you really *could* exert this kind of control over your life, you would have done so by now, somehow?

One way to accept life's uncertainty is to notice *spaces between* the things of life. The space between is home to the potential of the next moment. Three different levels for exploration:

- **"Big" spaces**—major life transitions—new job, moving to a new home, losing a relationship, or changes in seasons? How did you *respond* to the empty space created? fear, anxiety, relief, denial, joy, acceptance, anger? Did you rush to fill the void? Or did you slow down so as to notice more, learn and grow, and accept the natural ebb and flow of life?

- **"Medium" spaces**—moving *from* one activity *to* another, a task to a phone call, work to home, one thought to another. Were you annoyed, relieved, upset? What truly occurred *between* tasks?

- **"Small" spaces**—spaces between breaths, between thoughts. Might the tiny spaces in your life be openings to new possibility? Is this not, for example, the home of your intuition? Can you name what happens between your thoughts? In music, melody is about the spaces *between* notes.

We often think of a moment as being linear, having length, or breadth. We define *moment* as lasting a certain amount of time. Each moment also has *depth*. In its depth lives the opportunity we seek, the opportunity we miss as we skim the surface and see only the breadth.

PRINCIPLE #3: SELF-ORGANIZATION

"Man changes the conditions to suit the things. Nature changes the things to suit the conditions."
– John Burroughs

Summary: Life responds to *feedback*, an inherent attribute of all living systems, information within a system that guides its next steps. It's how creativity and opportunity unite to produce order from chaos, naturally. A personal culture of listening, inquiry and reflection offers a far more effective strategy for creating order than one based in command and control. *What if you could listen to, and implicitly trust, the clarity of your inner truth and your own experience to guide your next steps?*

Nature's Principle: Because everything is always becoming, and because uncertainty offers opportunity for creative expression, life's outcomes can't be planned in advance. Instead, life creates its next steps as it goes. And because nature's mind isn't already made up, choices are "context sensitive," responding to conditions *of* the moment, *in* the moment. She just keeps creating, regardless of what's happening. Yet here's the key: nature just keeps *listening*, too. What she hears is called *feedback.* It's an inherent attribute of all living systems. Every natural process, whether the inner workings of a human cell or birth and death of stars and galaxies, creates messages, real-time "status reports" about how things are going. With feedback, the creative process chooses what to do next. This approach generates far greater possibility than plans or goals could ever offer. (Goals presuppose one right path, leading to one right answer. Everything else is systematically missed.) Creativity and uncertainty together create order, naturally. Science calls these *complex adaptive systems*. The order we observe everywhere, from the spirals of a galaxy to the delicate figures of a snowflake, is just the adaptation of creativity to what's happening right now. Because creativity comes in many flavors and because conditions continually change, the universe is rich in variety. Chaos is nature's way of sustaining creativity. Self-organization is nature's way of creating order from chaos.

The Opening Offered: Although we've generally been taught otherwise, humans are complex, adaptive systems as well. Feedback is a naturally occurring phenomenon in our lives. It shows up concretely, in the results we experience, yet also intangibly, in the form of intuition, body sensations, emotions, imagination, dreams—aspects of ourselves we've learned to ignore in favor of "solid answers" from the external world. By shifting our awareness, however, through practices of quiet reflection, we open ourselves to hearing these messages so we might honor their truth. We might just find, as does nature, unlimited possibility in each moment. We also might discover, through personal experience, that our unconscious, life-long preference for a "command and control" approach to life simply hasn't served us so well, and that for far less effort and energy, we could experience so much more.

The principle of self-organization teaches us that we create our path in life by walking it, not by having it laid out ahead of time. Excellence, or mastery, then, comes not from "getting it right," but from living with intention and awareness our own unique gift of creative expression, learning and growing from each step along the way, wherever the way may lead. This creates a huge step into a life of personal authenticity.

Prevailing Wisdom: We are creatures of nature, guided by the same laws. But when we: shun creativity as unproductive, quell uncertainty to regain a lost sense of control, obsess on outcomes at the expense of the process that creates them, or invoke measurements from outside rather than listening to what's inside ... we fight life's natural flow, making "order" nearly impossible. We then wonder why life is so difficult! Despite the energy we put into planning how our lives, workplaces and relationships will turn out, we have little control over their outcomes. This leaves us stressed, disillusioned, even in despair. Afraid that letting go risks what little control we have, we instead hold even more tightly to the illusion, unaware it takes us just where we *don't* want to go.

The Opportunity/Promise: We need a shift in perspective: from *controlling* the moment to *responding in the moment.* Instead of obsessively measuring our lives, businesses or systems to see what's happening, we might instead listen to what these systems are already telling us through their feedback process. Classical measurement systems are akin to pulling up carrots in your garden to see how they're doing. Our lives and our world are too complex for us to understand; controlling them is impossible. A personal culture of listening, inquiry and reflection is a far more effective way to create order than one of command and control.

Nature's Story: If you've visited different areas of the world, you're aware of the unique "look and feel" of nature's places. Conditions are vastly different in the Pacific Northwest's rainforests than they are in Arizona's desert. Although the process is the same, the results are very different. Yet each ecosystem is ordered, designed around a unique environment and essence. Neither the stately cedar nor the lone saguaro cactus is upset that it doesn't grow somewhere else, or that it can't have less (or more) water. Each follows the elegant simplicity of the creative process, responding to feedback, and allowing it to unfold into order. Even in the midst of uncertainty, nature moves only toward what works.

My Story: On one hand, the story of how self-organization influenced my life is boring, simply because it's been experienced by many. On the other, it's crucial, for the long-term stranglehold this phenomenon has on so many is rarely resolved. Like many, I was brought up to get things right. Although not what I was taught, it is nevertheless what I learned and adopted. To me, getting A's became synonymous to being loved. Although I'm grateful for having the cerebral horsepower to do well, by the time I'd graduated from college, "perfection" was ingrained in me as an auto-pilot response to life. Society loves people who grew up like I did. As a Captain in the Air Force, I had ample opportunity to hone my skills. And as a young software engineer, I was rewarded well for working obsessively, unaware other choices existed. My "winning strategy" of being one who could fix anything had limits, however. I found two: 1) my wife didn't appreciate needing to be fixed, and 2) after inevitably being promoted to manager, employees failed to appreciate the impossible standards I set, and simply checked out.

I had my first personal coach in 1987. I didn't like him; he got in the way of my getting things right. But he was a master. Even clueless as I was (narcissists usually are), his words were to have such a profound impact on my life that I remember them word for word, despite the fact that they would take five years to germinate into action. "Brad, you may want to consider using your intellectual horsepower, not to get it right, but to *help others* get it right." In one sentence, he appealed to the perfectionist inside me and offered me a path forward, in an environment of respect and grace. Yet it took the loss of another marriage, a bunch of pissed-off employees and five years for me to see that controlling my world was not only futile, but that I'd created just what I *didn't* want. My world could be far more peaceful and productive by allowing instead of fighting.

An Invitation: What life rules have you adopted, perhaps in the name of "creating order," that *inhibit* the natural creativity and organizing ability life offers you? What's the price you pay for holding on? What if you didn't always have to have things "handled" or didn't have to "know?" Where do family, friends, co-workers, media, and society conspire to keep these outdated rules alive? How can you learn from each of life's experiences, including setbacks, rather than labeling and then trying to change them? Can you move with life's flow, listening to, and implicitly trusting, your own intention and felt experience of life to guide your next steps? How might your life change if, rather than controlling each moment, you used your innate capacity to *notice* more fully, and then *respond*—in each moment? How might you allow your own creativity to produce order out of chaos?

Practice: *Exploring the edges of your world.* The edges of your world are defined by your comfort zone—that which you've come to see as possible. The edges are made up of your life experiences and lessons. *Without* awareness of these stories, you unconsciously tend to retreat to the perceived safety of your comfort zone when you encounter something new. Being "on the edge" makes you uncomfortable. But when you live with awareness that these edges are a product of your mind, you can choose to stop, examine the edge, and see what it can teach you. Learning like this leads to growth—expansion of context.

The practice is *noticing.* Awareness does the work. Stop what you're doing several times a day. Envision yourself in the center of a field, the outer edges of which define your "known" world. Replay in your mind thoughts and events you've experienced since the last time you stopped. Allow each one to "test" how close you came to an edge. How long did you stay there? Did you unknowingly retreat to the perceived safety of the center? Did you *knowingly* retreat? What did you feel? What did you think? What might you have seen differently, had you been more aware? After some experience noticing, come to accept that your edges are unique to you, a perfect reflection of the thoughts and beliefs you hold. No need for judgment; just awareness that 1) "the way it is" *is*, and 2) your thinking is the causal factor in "the way it is." This opens up possibility, because as you *see* your thinking, your thinking changes.

The last part of this practice is this: begin to develop a new relationship with your edges. You've gone from unconscious retreat to conscious examination and learning; now it's time to try out something new—take a step outside your comfort zone. No need to "jump off the edge" here; it's about taking one step into new territory, with awareness that your other foot is on known ground. Try an experiment. Take a small step into unknown territory. As you experiment, ask yourself the same questions, about what you think and feel. Ask yourself what action you might take the next time you arrive at the same edge. In this way, your world, as represented by how you choose context, expands all on its own, often in dramatic ways.

PRINCIPLE #4: SIMULTANEITY

*"If you change the way you look at things,
the things you look at change."*
– Wayne Dyer

Summary: In nature, all possibility exists in each moment, "many right answers." Choosing one answer ahead of time, as with a goal, *limits* possibility, for it renders all others invisible from the start. You *create* more simply by learning to *see* more. In this sense, there is no independent reality; reality is a natural consequence of how you look at life. *What if you could dramatically expand the edges of your current perception, allowing your creative energy to fill the open space?*

Nature's Principle: In a universe that continually unfolds via creative expression, that senses and seizes opportunity when conditions allow, and that creates order from chaos, there must be an infinite number of possibilities from which to choose at any given moment. In fact, this is true; *all* possibilities always exist, *simultaneously*. The universe is alive with possibility. It's the place creativity goes when opportunity knocks. The world we see, whether this year or this instant, is simply that which has manifested out of an infinite sea of previous possibility. Other possibilities are still/always there, but are rendered invisible by the emergence of one specific choice. A simple analogy is this: a crow flies past you; it has an infinite number of choices where it can fly next, in every instant. As it chooses one path, all the paths it *didn't* take become invisible. At the same time, an infinite number of new paths continue to emerge in the next instant, and the next.

Quantum science has taken this principle a step further, showing that an observer of a system impacts the behavior of the system.

Example: light is made up of photons; photons can exhibit both particle-like and wave-like tendencies. The *possibility* to be either is always there. The simple act of observation, however, results in a photon "choosing" to manifest as one or the other; a curious result, with very interesting consequences, as we shall see; infinite possibility, manifesting anew in each instant.

The Opening Offered: Although we've learned to love having answers, especially instant ones, the principle of simultaneity suggests we'd be better off staying with questions instead, at least for longer periods of time. As soon as we have an answer, *other* possible answers, which were always there, vanish from view. Curiously, once we have an answer, we also stop thinking. As with a crow's flight, there are always "many right answers." We therefore have potential to *create* more just by being open to more. As we see more, possibilities emerge; with continued awareness and openness, they keep materializing with every step.

Non-dualism is a term often used to describe the idea that nothing is "separate" from the whole, that there's truly no right/wrong, either/or, good/bad, except in our perception of it. This is one way in which simultaneity plays out in our lives. All things are, in some way, both. Dualism (exclusively one *or* the other) does not truly exist. By learning to see both-ness in everything, we come to appreciate simultaneity and the power of many right answers. This, in turn, opens us to seeing with a "consciousness of possibility." Every moment is alive with potential.

Prevailing Wisdom: As a society, we've become obsessed by having answers. Society's systems, from families to schools to businesses to institutions, seem to value "one right answer" above all. Among other things, this is home for fundamentalist thinking—the idea that, with only one answer, there's no more conversation. It's also the home for our obsession with setting goals, the way to *achieve* that one right answer. Goals, however, can create more problems than they solve. Setting a goal is not only to declare, "there's one right answer," but it's also a way of defining the answer before setting out on the creative process from which it manifests. That's not only stifling, but it causes us to systematically ignore all other possibilities we encounter along the way, which nature tells us are infinite in number. We wonder why life often feels so constraining, unaware that our ways of seeing and thinking created the constraints. This is why a shift in how we see and think offers such a powerful path forward.

The Opportunity/Promise: In a world that is susceptible to the power of thinking and seeing, there is no such thing as "independent reality." We *create* our reality by how we see and think. Because the universe is far too complex for us to comprehend, we're accustomed to seeing what we look for instead of what's there. Simultaneity tells us the more we "see for possibility," the more possibility we'll see. This is how two people presented with identical information can arrive at different conclusions. Again, we can create more by learning to see more. This demonstrates the value in defining the framework, or context, of our lives, and not worrying so much about the details or the content. By creating bigger and bigger contexts, we simple *allow* bigger and bigger realities to fill them.

Nature's Story: A beautiful example of simultaneity in nature is the "braided stream," a river flowing in a broad, flat valley, which allows the flow to separate into many channels that continually crisscross, so as to appear from above as a braid. Its beauty and complexity come from the fact that it is both one river and many rivers, simultaneously. If we view a piece of the stream up close, we have the sense we're looking at a river. Looking at another piece of the stream, we again see "a river." Yet when we climb the banks and gaze from a broader perspective, the whole comes into view. We see "both-ness," one and many, together. We're like this too. Personality is a braided stream, one person, but with many personalities, expressed at different times and different ways.

My Story: My engineer personality has been a force in shaping my life. Get it right; be responsible; fix it all; be perfect. I'd always thought this was my winning strategy. Lots of things in the world needed to be fixed. Managers loved me; the bait they offered showed up as goals. Engineers love goals; I was no exception. Goals are business language for "one right answer." The engineer was my way of saying *yes* to goals, a perfect, if not dysfunctional, pair. I brute-forced my way through 25 years of business life, unaware I'd missed probably 90% of the opportunity life held for me, the *other* right answers; I was too busy pursuing just one. I'd also left behind a wake of those I'd walked on, disrespected or ignored. I feel sad—for missed opportunity and for the wake I left behind.

It took the loss, in a single year, of all I'd been *taught* I should work a lifetime for—my job, professional reputation, a marriage, a home, and a retirement account—for me to even notice this was happening. I recall waking up mornings wondering who I was; all I *thought* defined me was gone—a painful opening to a world of many right answers.

Nothing in my previous ways of seeing offered me any help; I was in foreign territory. I recalled what I'd learned about being lost in the wilderness. Step 1: Stop and think; it's not the time for panic. We're at our greatest risk of failure when we continue to rely on what has worked in the past. Step 2: Look around. The environment always offers feedback, clues to next steps. Step 3: Follow clues, not old ways of thinking. In wilderness, a choice to walk downhill and/or follow a stream is a better strategy than walking uphill, no matter what your mind says, as streams end up in the sea. I stopped and looked around. Although I was tempted to ask for help (a decidedly new idea for me), I noticed everyone else looked lost, too. Then, for a reason I still can't explain logically, it dawned on me I'd looked at only half my world, the outside. I'd never looked inside myself for clues to anything. Scary as it was to look inside, I had another unexplainable revelation: if my engineer personality could be that good at solving anything in the outside world, how about putting him to work figuring out my inner world. He discovered what sages have known for centuries, and what I'd never realized consciously until then, that everything I'd ever done or thought or said in life had come from a belief system that was acting as a "conveyor belt," unconsciously ferrying outdated and false lessons into my world as "truth," and I'd been "listening" all these years. Another big opening.

Invitation: How often do you forsake the experience of the journey for the promise of the destination? When you "get there," how do you deal with the inevitable letdown of the failed promise? How might your life change by changing how you see? What do you see when you "look at" life? Abundance or scarcity, judgment or learning, fear or love, possibility or boundaries? What if, in a world of diverging viewpoints, one of them didn't have to be *wrong*? Take a step back; ask yourself how the view, and therefore the answer, changes. Wherever you've adopted a rigid structure around your life, you've clouded your perception and made *lack* of possibility self-fulfilling prophecy. Explore "in between." Ambiguity opens you to new possibilities— remember "Principle #2—Opportunism." You not only create your own journey, but your own map, too. If possibility isn't on your map, you can't go there.

Practice: *Envisioning a Thriving Future.* If the world is filled with possibilities, then you must be able to manifest one that matches your deepest longing, right? By using imagination to "see" potential ahead of you, you can "dream a world into being." Although another of those skills you learn to deny early in life, placing imaginative attention on what you love actually allows it to *emerge* out of the countless possibilities available. Remember: your thinking is a causal factor in your reality.

Envision your ideal life as a movie, with the "you" discovered in practices above. Imagine yourself living a life of your dreams, one that evokes the heart, soul and spirit of the deep personal truth you may have never dared to expose, even to yourself. Pretend you're the director of your movie—because you *are*! As a director knows, *anything* can come next. You change the script, creating a story that evokes your greatest potential. *This is not about planning or predicting a future, but about giving your dreams energy, 'space' for them to manifest.* The unconscious mind has no concept of past or future, or of reality or imagination. It hears only what gets repeatedly put into it. As you practice envisioning a great life, you "create a memory of the future," so as you step into it, your mind no longer sees it as a scary place ... it already sees it as home. This isn't Hollywood: no need to sell 50 million copies; just one—to yourself.

PRINCIPLE #5: RHYTHM

"All rivers run to the sea, yet the sea is not full."
– Ecclesiastes 1:7

Summary: Underneath its surface chaos, life is incomprehensible order. Life's natural patterns offer far more meaning than the events comprising them. Birth and death, abundance and dearth, quiet space between. Without one, there is no other. Without emptiness, there is no room for new creation. Cycles are nature's way to renew and refresh. *What if you could graciously accept life's ups and downs, living more deeply in "the space between," opening without judgment to lessons of both peaks and valleys?*

Nature's Principle: As is now clear, there's order throughout the universe. Life sustains itself and its order because the process of creative expression acts in cycles, or rhythms, not discrete events alone. In this way, nature's process ensures the continual renewal of life, cycle upon cycle of recurring rhythms that define everything. Three crucial attributes of rhythms surface: 1) One aspect of a cycle is no better or worse than another; they're equal partners in *becoming*. Summer and winter don't argue; high tide doesn't fight with low. 2) *Time* is of no concern to cycles; each works according to its essence, not to external schedules or plans. Hummingbirds beat their wings hundreds of times per minute. Day and night create a 24-hour cycle, one rotation of earth. Volcanoes build mountains; rain, wind and waves wear them down, a cycle spanning millions of years. The birth and death of stars is a cycle billions of years long. None is worried about being done sooner or taking too long. 3) *Meaning* is found in the nature of the pattern itself, not in the events that comprise it. If trees didn't refresh leaves or needles, they'd not last too long. As old stars explode, they offer material to create new ones. If earth didn't spin on its axis, we'd not have days or nights. If it didn't revolve around the sun, we'd not have seasons ... or perhaps weather.

Nature's rhythms and patterns happen not only at all scales of time, microseconds to eons, but also at all levels of energy. We're used to patterns we can perceive with our senses, but many natural rhythms can't be perceived in this way. Birds fly in formation, and fish swim in schools, with patterns defining their motions; there's simply no way group members could "get the message" using only basic senses.

The Opening Offered: As in nature, our lives are made up of naturally occurring cycles that also form patterns: dearth/ abundance, ebb/flow, birth/death. Whether about jobs, money, relationships, health or emotion, life is rhythm. Life's patterns are our best teachers, showing us what we need to learn. While they create both order *and* chaos, they're also the home of balance. In fact, we experience recurring cycles because often we learn only with repetition; repetition happens until we learn. We fail to appreciate the impact of natural patterns in our lives because they operate with a subtlety or over time periods that preclude easy observation. Only after we've repeatedly experienced *effects* of life's patterns do we become aware of their *causes*. By learning to recognize, accept, then join the natural flow of life's rhythms, we align our lives with the underlying order and balance we see everywhere in nature.

Prevailing Wisdom: Impatient as we've become for instant results and gratification, we fret more over controlling *what isn't* than noticing *what is*. So we fragment life into pieces, leaving us with a belief that at least we can control something. Nature, however, tells us when we remove anything from its context, we rob it of its meaning. We can truly know a thing only through its wholeness. Fragmentation leads not to knowledge but to judgment, which leads us to false conclusions. Life isn't that simple; our attempts to control it are futile. The energy that drives life's patterns holds far more power than our will. We've come to want only the "good" in life's patterns, so we often design our lives around avoiding the "bad." Meaning is found in the pattern's richness, not in any judgment we make as to whether it's good or bad. Life's highs exist only in relation to its lows.

The Opportunity/Promise: Complexity and chaos only thinly veil the majesty of the natural order below, an order sustained by rhythm. As a way to find that order, and align our lives with it, the most useful tool available to us is *awareness*. If we approached life through the lens of pattern recognition rather than judgment, we'd find the balance and meaning we want, with far less effort. As we begin to notice this way, another powerful tool is *acceptance*. Accepting what we *can't* control, we allow life's natural rhythms to do their work on us, so we can join their flow, saving our precious energy for things we *can* control, such as our awareness, level of consciousness, how we see and think.

Nature's Story: Of all nature's rhythms here on earth, the annual cycle of the seasons seems to have the greatest impact on us. Seasons are a combined effect of the revolution of the earth around the sun and the earth's tilt on its axis. Over the course of a year, the earth continuously presents a changing face to the sun. Varying amounts of sunlight cause the changes we experience as seasons. Seasons vary little in the tropics, where the amount of sunshine is rather constant throughout the year. In fact, nighttime is more of a season in the tropics than is winter. In temperate latitudes, seasonal differences can be pronounced.

As seasons create a rhythm of their own, they also create openings for cycles of life's renewal, rhythm on top of rhythm. Plants and animals synchronize their life cycles to passage of the seasons. Hummingbirds migrate north from the tropics each spring; blossoming of plants along their entire route is timed so as to allow hummingbirds to pollinate the flowers. Which adaptation came first, bird or plant, is meaningless; the *pattern* is the carrier of meaning. For us, however, seasonal rhythms are more likely to evoke complaint than adaptation. Curiously, I've never heard a complaint about winter that delayed its arrival.

My Story: My life, too, has been marked by seasons. Each offered me an opportunity to grow, had I been able to notice recurring patterns. Whether with relationships, jobs, finances or new ideas, I was offered much yet noticed little. This persisted for over 25 years of adult life.

An example: At 47, I'd been divorced three times. Although I cherished each relationship, I realized I'd created a story about shortcomings of each. Somehow, the stories brought me a sense of peace. What I didn't realize then was that this feeling of peace came more from my story than from reality. A year after the third, I began to see from a different perspective. Instead of finding what was *different* about each relationship, I looked for what they had in *common*. The unsettling answer was all too clear: *Me!* From this disquieting and somewhat scary opening, I began to see the previous 24 years as a pattern, recurring events with a message. I'd entered each relationship, in part, to fill a void (that I *needed* to be loved). When each failed, (I was playing out my issues instead of being in relationship), I filled the void, unaware I was re-creating a pattern, more of the same. Finally, able to see, my feelings shifted from anger and righteousness to sadness and regret. I also began to notice an even larger pattern, one superimposed on this relationship pattern. I realized I'd brought the same "command and control" consciousness to everything I touched, not just relationships, but my work, the building of my home, and in a way, even parenting my two sons.

After another few years of inquiry, an even broader perspective offered me the real lesson: I needed to find love in myself if I were to share it with another, and that I could never resolve childhood issues through an adult relationship. With that, sadness and regret gave way to acceptance and gratitude—that it all happened for a reason and I'd finally learned.

An Invitation: Do you greet life's natural cycles with acceptance and learning, or with resistance? For each of life's events, can you discover the pattern to which the event belongs? Where are the *edges* of patterns you accept with grace, compared to ones you fight? What changes would allow you to become more accepting of patterns, large and small?

Practice: *Joining the rhythm of life's flow.* A great way to notice patterns is to trace them over the course of a lifetime. It's an antidote to our obsession with details, and our habit of ascribing to them a level of significance far greater than the part they truly play in our lives. Tonight, you will be the *audience* at a movie you've starred in for years, yet may not know so well— your own. Create quiet time and space for yourself, without distraction. Re-play your life story in broad-brush terms. Start with a snapshot in your mind, depicting how you see your life up until now. Then review big themes that run through your life. Go back as far as you can; it's a full-length movie. Notice the *significance* you attach to some things (and not to others). Notice how you weave a *story* about your life, how the story differs from the simple facts and events that comprise it. No judgment here; just noticing, clarity, honesty. Look for places where you repeated the same thing, albeit in different ways.

Do this exercise *several* times over days or weeks, filling in blanks as experiences and feelings come back to you. Notice judgments you make—about yourself, others, how you live. For now, don't "judge the judgments." As observer, you notice what you missed while being the star. You may see themes superimposed on life's events, *recurring patterns.* Ask yourself what common aspects unite the patterns you observe, and what might be different for you if you *knew* that the true meaning in your life had been about the patterns, not the events. It matters less that you "like" what you see than you "see what is so."

Just as in nature, patterns create the story of life. Nothing is either/or, but both/and. In your own life, if you fight *both/and* to seek the apparent comfort of *either/or*, you're interrupting life's natural flow. A paradox of being human is that we live in the space *between* "a" and "b." "A" exists only in *relationship* to "b." Happy lives only in contrast to sad. If you fight off pain, you unknowingly fight off joy. Both-ness.

Last, use your new "pattern recognition" consciousness to ask how you might better notice, then interpret, tomorrow's events so as to honor their place in life's natural, yet paradoxical, both-ness, and allow those patterns to guide your life from a larger perspective than you do today.

PRINCIPLE #6: ENERGY

*"The more you lose yourself in something bigger
than yourself, the more energy you will have."*
– Norman Vincent Peale

Summary: The unifying force in the universe is energy. Time and space are simply by-products of how energy manifests. Energy goes only into sustaining the process of creation—a process of elegant simplicity with manifestations that are miraculously complex and diverse. *How do you use your energy—to create a life you'd love or to fight the one you've got? What if your awareness were so keen that you could devote energy only to what matters most … your creative essence?*

Nature's Principle: Energy defines the *unity* in the universe. At the instant of the Big Bang, only energy existed. All matter manifested from that singular energy, each according to its own unique creative essence. Total energy in the universe is therefore constant; it can be transformed into matter and back again, but neither created nor destroyed. The result is a remarkably resilient, sustainable and elegantly beautiful world. Energy always goes into creating; nothing is wasted. Whether we experience energy in the form of light, a volcano, a star, a human being or a table, it is all one. Because nature's principles are held together by this single source, some of the words here may sound familiar. Such is the nature of oneness, the energy behind the underlying order of everything. In an energetic universe, all other aspects of life are "by-products." Time, space, and even matter are simply *results* of how energy manifests.

In our more "local" universe here on earth, the sun is our source of energy. Itself a remnant of the Big Bang, it maintains temperatures conducive to all life as we know it. It powers photosynthesis, where solar energy is transformed into food energy to sustain plant life, and in turn, all life on earth. No matter how we look at life on earth, we can draw a straight line from any of its manifestations back to the sun as its source.

The Opening Offered: Our physical world is tangible, perceived with the five senses. The energy that shapes that world, however, is invisible. Constantly at work, it organizes information, creating our experience of life. We gain glimpses into this energy in the form of intuition, synchronistic experiences, visions and dreams, but largely it's at work behind the scenes, creating order from chaos. As we grow in awareness and in new ways of seeing, we gain access to the inner workings of energy in our lives and can tap it in the service of our greatest potential.

Each of us has a unique reason for being here, our natural essence, the part of self that wants to express itself in how we choose to live, a way to honor our life's greatest potential or soul's purpose. It's where life "wants" us to devote our energy. As we discover this authentic truth, we have a choice to honor its fulfillment. In doing so, we open ourselves to the underlying order and flow of nature's way to guide us. Life's energy equation then shifts toward one of meaning, balance and sustainability. This expands our sense of time, allowing the energy of our truth to fill the space provided. We live "in the flow."

Prevailing Wisdom: When we complain that our lives don't work, we often identify the enemies as time, money, job, relationship, even luck. Because we've come to believe these things have power, we've grown to fear them. So we then had to create all manner of elaborate structures to keep their power in check. By identifying them as enemies, however, we create a hostile environment, which of course requires us to fight—to win a battle we made up in our heads. We even see signs of winning this fight as proof that we're truly alive, when all we're really doing is draining energy. Curiously, the only aspect of life we *can* control is the one in *limited* supply—energy. If we use it on negative thoughts, we've got little left for positive ones. It's that simple, and it's a choice. Two problems hold us back here: 1) We don't know what matters most to us. Think of it as "intention deficit disorder", and 2) We're unaware that the key to living our truth is the choice of how we manage energy. As a result, we get sidetracked a lot.

The Opportunity/Promise: When you discover the authentic truth living inside you and begin to consciously devote your life energy to what matters to you, the way you experience life changes dramatically. As you devote your energy to what truly matters, you experience more enjoyment. As you do, time seems to disappear. From loving yourself more, connections with others and with the world deepen. With deeper connection comes an opening to the depths of your own consciousness; you tap the natural energies of intuition, imagination and spirit. True meaning comes from your own internal experience of life, not from any external thing or measurement. You will have created a sense of meaning that is uniquely and powerfully your own.

Nature's Story: Spruce trees don't get mad that's it's too cold during winter. A nautilus doesn't worry about the shape of its shell. Yet each is miraculously, beautifully tailored to be exactly what it is. Nature's processes and principles are simple, yet the manifestations are infinitely complex. By putting energy only into expressing its own essence, every organism contributes to its ecological niche and nurtures its sustainability. Elegant simplicity. Humans, however, are different. We're unique in the sense that we can choose to *ignore* our essence and try to live someone else's instead. And we wonder why we're often dissatisfied.

An example of conflict between the human dilemma and nature's way is the story of the U.S. Army Corps of Engineers vs. the Mississippi River. Rivers are alive; we might best think of the word *river* as a verb; a river is a process, not a result. If it stopped flowing and became just a result, it would no longer be a river. A river's essence is to move water along a least-energy path from land to sea. The least-energy path is rarely a straight line (a life-lesson all its own). If a river encounters rocks impeding its flow, it finds a new path. "Offending" rocks let the river know; the river responds. No summit meeting; no project plan; no attitude; no denial. Even without rocks, rivers tend to meander; it's their way of finding lower-energy pathways. If the Corps of Engineers accepted how rivers do this, they'd stop trying to make the Mississippi River go where it doesn't want to go. The river's "intention," by the way, informed by its own feedback, says there's a lower-energy path to the Gulf of Mexico than by way of New Orleans. That path is to join the Atchafalaya River a few hundred miles north. The problem is that nature's way has been deemed "inconvenient" by the Corps, hence billions of dollars spent trying to control the river. In the long run, any attempt to change the flow of the Mississippi River is futile. For the engineers, it's an issue of *drama*, that there's something wrong with the river's course that needs to be fixed. For the river, it's about *possibility*, that there's a lower-energy path to the sea. Unlike us, nature loves to find easy ways to do things. Furthermore, nature can't *not* do this; she will always find the lowest energy path, always find new possibilities. I'm not sure why that idea seems to so confound the Corps of Engineers. Of this I *am* sure: the river passes no judgment on those who would try to mess with it.

My Story: I now see how much energy I've wasted in life, trying to right things that weren't wrong, plan things that were unpredictable, control things that can't be controlled. Science told me there is always a least-energy path. Science did *not* tell me how nature found this path against a backdrop of unity, wholeness and allowing, rather than a backdrop of fragments, scheming and force ... creations of my mind. I brute-forced a lot of results, simply due to my myopic view on energy.

An Invitation: Does your energy go into creating the life you want, or into to fighting the one you've got? What if you designed your entire life around the expression of your unique essence? How could the simplicity of living your essence open you to a much larger experience of life? What if life's meaning could show up naturally, just from being your true self? What if time no longer mattered because you "had it all?" What if you accepted complete personal responsibility for the reality you have created? Big questions; not easy answers. Life's a journey.

Practice: *Manifesting your vision.* We tend to see *time* as life's most precious commodity. "If I only had more time, then ..." Yet each of us has 24 hours a day, the same as those we hold in high regard as being especially productive—Gandhi, Michelangelo, Einstein or Mother Teresa. What set them apart was a level of clarity about what mattered, so they devoted more energy to what mattered and less to what *didn't*. Life's precious commodity is *energy*. This is why envisioning a thriving future is powerful; energy you put into your vision creates a "memory of the future," so when you take a step into it, it no longer feels unknown, scary. Your mind "knows it as home." You're "pulled" into it.

Take one step into possibility each day. It doesn't matter if the step is big or small, or even what the step is, as long as it honors your truth, and that you take it with intention. Do one thing each day that evokes the real you. A few curious things will happen. After each step, you're afforded a new view—how things look *after* you've taken your step. Every step into new possibility creates a new view. As you stop, just look around. Listen. No more goals, plans, agendas, forcing, control or stress. Take a step, then stop and listen. Allow life's natural feedback to guide your next steps. If feedback tells you to edit your vision a bit, do it. It's your life; you can steer it in any direction you wish. Why choose a direction that doesn't work when the information you need to choose wisely is right there in front of you?

As part of your self-observation, notice where your "daily allotment" of energy goes. See how much went to your authentic truth and how much was lost on worry, anxiety, stress, social acceptance or guilt.

You may now see that three ingredients, folded together through the practice of becoming them, define your recipe for a remarkable future: 1) *non-judgmental* and *conscious awareness* of what's going on right now; 2) acceptance of, and trust in, your *innate creative genius* (who you truly are; what matters most to you); 3) *feedback,* the natural information flow inherent in life's experience that tells you how things are going; feedback guides your next steps.

PRINCIPLE #7: COMMUNITY

"A healthy social life is found only when, in the mirror of each
soul, the whole community finds its reflection, and when,
in the whole community, the virtue of each one is living."
– Rudolph Steiner

Summary: Survival and sustainability favor cooperation and collaboration, through the creation of adaptive and resilient systems of order—from galaxies to ecosystems to organisms to atoms—communities built around a common thread. Everything occurs "in relationship." Shared visions create energy that reinforces the essence of both individual and collective. *What if your connection with others could create a "spiral of possibility" around you, bringing out the best in yourself and in others?*

Nature's Principle: Creative expression drives the universe, each thing according to its own essence. From one perspective, essence is about embodying one's uniqueness, and in so doing, surviving and sustaining that uniqueness. It might appear as if this process would lead to heavy competition. While competition exists over needed resources (such as sunlight and water), it's an exception in the bigger picture. Long-term sustainability favors cooperation, which happens through the principle of self-organization, via the development of *communities*. A community is an adaptive, resilient system of order designed around a common thread. Communities thrive by developing an essence all their own, then living that creative essence following the same principles as the organisms comprising it. Communities, then, are ecosystems. Once again, nature becomes ordered no matter at what level or scale we observe it.

Far from being static, mechanistic collections of processes and parts, communities are living systems. From subatomic particles, pieces build into larger wholes—elements, molecules, organisms—each a community, each part of a still larger community. Communities culminate in the oneness of the universe, as the next and last principle will show.

The Opening Offered: As in nature, cooperation and collaboration add value, sustainability and balance to our lives. Community building offers a far more effective strategy for living authentically and making a difference than the more pervasive strategies of competition, command and control. The latter leads to scarcity thinking, greed and fear, while the former leads to creative genius, possibility and abundance.

Everything we do is done in relationship; nothing stands on its own. We might think of our activities as conversations (even those we have with ourselves), each one a community that supports us in a meaningful way. We consciously choose some of our communities—friends, jobs, spouses, religious institutions. Some we don't think of as communities, yet join them anyway, by using them—roads, phones, internet, stores, banks. The point is that we don't do much alone, despite lessons that we need to be in control and not ask for help. Our consciously chosen communities are built around the common threads of our own essence. Holding a collective vision of what's possible helps to focus energy, which allows both community and individual to move forward. By helping to reinforce who we are together, communities reinforce who we are as individuals at the same time. It's about *inter*dependence.

Prevailing Wisdom: We're taught to do it all and be in control, under the guise of being personally responsible. It doesn't work. None of us survives as an island. While we may resist or reject the support and synergy communities offer, we can't live without them. Thoreau may stand as an icon of individualist spirit, living as he did in a cabin at Walden Pond. But it didn't take him all that long to walk into town, where he had dinner with his mother more often than not. Our fight with the notion of community, and the perceived threat it creates under the heading of vulnerability, has kept us from embracing the power relationships truly hold. Adaptable, self-determining systems encourage creative genius; command and control systems encourage only compliance.

The Opportunity/Promise: As in nature, a few simple principles could lead us toward community with neither agenda nor struggle. In healthy communities, life's energy flows naturally; we expand as we allow our own energy to merge with this flow. It's a way we can use ordinary means to create extraordinary results. Community building transforms the power of "me" into "we." Original cultures knew this well. Perhaps because they had no written language, community was the carrier of culture, story was the teacher, and experiences of nature wove the tapestry from which stories unfolded. Story guided individuals to know they were part of something bigger, and thereby develop both a strong sense of self and a commitment to the well-being of the whole. This reverent and reciprocal relationship with nature was not only a way of life but also a system of faith, a contributor to their sustainability.

Nature's Story: For at least six months each year, the Canadian Arctic is a study in white: a generally featureless land covered with snow, under leaden skies, wind chill adding to its austerity and hostility. Above the latitude of the tree line, it's often difficult to know where land stops and sky begins. On some days, it's downright impossible. Of the seven bird species living there year-round, only the raven is black. If snow arrives late one year, the now-white willow ptarmigan (a quail relative) and arctic fox are easy targets for prey. This is the community of the tundra, the ecosystem of the far north. It holds together around a common theme—cold, snow, extremes. Everything is well adapted to these extremes, however. Polar bears, for example, overheat 13 times as fast as humans at a walking pace, serving them well here but not at temperatures above freezing. To share time and space with those who call this place home evokes a sense of wonder and awe at the miracle of nature's communities. Yet every aspect of this community follows the same principles as does every aspect of other communities, vastly different manifestations, a single set of principles and the same processes at work. Consistency, yet not sameness, at every level.

My Story: In the early 1990s, I returned to graduate school to pursue a master's degree in environmental studies. I'd been lured by my life-long love of nature, and my now-emerging sense of a bigger personal life, as some of these stories portray. I'd had it in my head to use my business background to lead nature tours, offering others adventure and education in a world that needed nurture. As a part of my studies, I did an internship, helping an acquaintance who operated a nature photography tour company. He told me if I could handle the logistical rigor of their arctic tours, I could do anything. So I went to Canada's Arctic to learn the polar bear tour business. As an engineer, logistics wouldn't scare me as they did him, and I was excited about the opportunity to see a part of the world about which I'd always dreamed. Days were short in November; wind chills of minus 40 degrees were common; sunlight was not. I loved it; fascinated by how this place even worked at all. I began leading tours on my own the year after this, an avocation that stayed with me for 20 years. I have taken hundreds of adventurers to see polar bears.

The first few years were scary for me; I was in the company of leaders who ranked as top bear biologists, nature photographers and Arctic historians in North America. Who was I to lead tours such as these? During the long evenings, participants commonly gathered with their group for conversation and community. Curiously, I noticed people from other groups often hung out with me instead of with their own group and leaders. One evening, I asked one woman why. Her response startled me: "We came to experience the Arctic as a community, not to learn bear biology, and only you are offering this conversation." Reflecting later on her words, I realized I was simply being "me." Not one of us was a "better" tour leader. As for me, however, I learned a great deal about who I was and the value my authentic self offered to others.

An Invitation: Where are the walls in your life? What are you walling in, or out? What do you gain, or lose, with your walls? How does your connection to something bigger help serve the greater good? How does the whole then contribute to *your* growth? Stepping further back, what is your unique place in the universe? How do you talk about this, with yourself, others, in community? How does your connection with others create a "spiral of possibility" around you, one that makes your contribution in the world far greater than you could possibly make alone?

Practice: *Toward reverent and reciprocal dialogue.* We do everything "in relationship," with something or someone else. Even the staunchest of "I do everything on my own" believers are members of many communities. In this practice, I suggest growing your connections with others, centered around the ideas of *story* and *dialogue*.

Story: one way to view yourself and your life is as a story. Practices using the *movie idea* are examples. Over the course of your life, you live, tell, and create a story. To the extent your stories are congruent, you experience integrity. Review each day through the lens of *story*. What story did you *live*? What story did you *tell*? Do you tell the same story everywhere? Do you *believe* your story? Lastly, what story are you *creating* about how tomorrow will be for you? How does your "tomorrow" story influence the way "tomorrow" turns out? Your story is woven from threads of your life experience and consciousness.

Dialogue: Dialogue is an open, two-way exchange based in reverence and respect, with an intention that both parties learn and grow. It's far different from the conflict-laden, sound-bite chatter or one-way monologues common in our lives today. Review connections with your communities through the lens of *dialogue*. Whether it's work, family, service or religion, name a common thread/purpose this community stands for. Ask yourself if the conversations of this community fit the above definition of dialogue. Do they support or enhance the common purpose you identified? What does the community gain by your presence? What do you gain by belonging? What does either lose? Does the community completely accept you for who you are, thereby empowering you to be your best, unique self? Does it do the same with others? Do you accept others completely and empower them to be their best as well? These are heavy questions. Not even the most thriving communities always fit these ideals; yet they help you understand how mutually-enhancing your communities are (or not). They also help you to understand yourself in new ways, and how associations contribute to your life and well-being. By the way, if they don't contribute, you're free to release membership, and choose something that makes your life work better instead.

PRINCIPLE #8: CONNECTEDNESS

"I am a part of all that I have met."
– Alfred Lord Tennyson

Summary: Everything in the universe is inextricably connected to everything else. Nothing survives as a fragment. We are united by the original energy of creation. The entire universe, therefore, is contained in every piece, no matter how small—as in a hologram. Extracting pieces from their context under the guise of getting to know them has robbed life of its wholeness, and therefore its source of meaning. *What if you knew that how you see, think, speak and act has a profound effect, not only on your life, but on the lives of everything and everyone else, too?*

Nature's Principle: Fourteen billion years ago, the universe sprang into being with a flash of energy, energy that to this day powers *all* of nature's creative processes. Due to that singular event, everything in the universe always has been, is now, and always will be, inextricably connected to everything else. Whether matter or energy, animate or inanimate, visible or not, everything we know is the current manifestation of energy from the universe's creation. Because energy manifests in different ways and rates, we *experience* things as separate, when in fact, they are truly all one. Therefore, any action by *any* thing affects *every* thing. The mere presence of an organism affects every other organism. Opportunity, therefore, unfolds from the unity of the whole, a web of infinite possibility. Meaning derives not from details or individual events, but from the *context* in which those events exist—a context of wholeness, or unity. In order to know a thing, we have to know what it's connected to, because *connectedness* is one of its attributes. Nothing survives as a fragment; everything is "context sensitive."

It's impossible for our minds to fully grasp the significance of life's mystery; in fact, all we really can do is observe it. One conclusion we *can* draw, however, is that life is not the straight line, cause-and-effect system we learned in school. It's a miraculous, often-unpredictable, complex, *web* of interconnectedness. Quantum science has taken the principle of connectedness a step further, with concepts such as *non-locality*, which asserts that energy connections can span the entire universe, in an instant. This idea of "action at a distance" violates our classical-science-based, cause-and-effect learning. Yet its truth asks us to see life as a unified whole, everything already and always connected.

The Opening Offered: The interconnectedness of absolutely everything means that our struggles, be they sadness, complexity, chaos, uncertainty or fear—are inextricably tied to everything *else* in life. Chaos is part of wholeness, not something we rip apart from its surroundings to make us feel better, or worse. This offers a phenomenal opening; it's not life or the world that creates the problems we experience, but rather *how we see and think about* life and the world. Only by changing the way we believe, see and think—about ourselves, others, life, and the world—can we bring inside our frame or view that which we formerly thought was separate from us, and therefore in need of our control. The key to expanding our perspective is to see everything for the interconnectedness it is, and in the process come to accept that we cannot possibly know it all (and that it's ok we don't).

Prevailing Wisdom: We've learned we need to be in control of our lives. Unaware it's futile, we adopt all kinds of elaborate beliefs and behaviors to give us a *false* sense of certainty, in a world inherently uncertain by design. Even the classical science we learned in school encourages, even depends upon, breaking the world into pieces, getting to know the pieces, feeling we control something, then moving to the next piece; keep repeating throughout life. It's a compensation strategy for our unwillingness to accept the uncertainty and complexity of wholeness as a fact of life. The idea is so ingrained, however, that we fail to see that it has caused more problems for us than the uncertainty it attempts to eliminate. We've gone so far as to disconnect ourselves from soul, spirit, feeling and intuition, just to "be in control." Then we wonder why we feel lost and disillusioned.

The Opportunity/Promise: Our true potential lies in knowing that every belief, thought, word or action makes a difference—whether positive or negative, whether intentional or not. Too complex to be fully grasped, the idea is not too complex, however, to be fully experienced. By seeing and allowing connectedness, we start to discover that meaning comes from life's *context*, not from its day-to-day situations. By *seeing* meaning in a new way, we *create* meaning in a new way. And by feeling the connectedness that just *is*, we have a natural antidote to the loneliness and despair that permeate our society. Looking at the principles of connectedness and simultaneity together, we see that all possibilities not only exist in each moment, but are completely connected to each other in an infinite sea called the "field of potential." We create order out of that chaos with our perception, bringing one possibility into reality with our intention, thereby giving life its meaning.

Nature's Story: Between 6,000 and 10,000 years ago, the latest cycle of glaciation drew to a close. As the up-to-9,000-foot-thick ice receded, it exposed a land scraped clean of life. From the south came lichen, the pioneers that colonize newly exposed land. A combination of algae and fungus, lichen is a community, built around common purpose. The algae provides a food source through photosynthesis; and the fungus provides for a structure—a place to live. Lichen colonize bare rock; over hundreds of years, they work their way into cracks, breaking rocks apart, the first step in the formation of soil. In time, there's enough soil to support plants unable to live on bare rock, yet now at home in a newly emerging landscape. Millennia pass; plants grow and die, decay releases nutrients, creating more soil. Eventually, forests cover the land, as we see today across central Canada. Forest and land become home to more plants, birds and animals, suited to a changing landscape. This ecosystem is a community, too, self-organized out of the myriad choices available, nature having stepped into the opportunities offered, one after another. A single tree in this forest never stands alone. It's part of, and inextricably tied to, soil, nutrients, water, and ultimately to solar energy that powers the process. Trees themselves come and go, with rhythm that never stops, only the process that creates them being sustained. The forest we see today is both the same forest and a very different forest from the one we'd see hundreds of years hence. Connectedness. All is one.

My Story: Although connectedness is evident everywhere, I need to remain aware of it lest I get caught in the trap of separateness that defines our world. When immersed in "life as story," I hold life more sacred, so I notice more. I once had the opportunity to be part of a Native American tradition of connectedness. Their premise: personal culture, the carrier of meaning (I call it *context* in this book), can be viewed as an invisible container, a basket woven of threads of experience—connectedness to land, family, sense of self and place in the world. It's up to each of us to weave our own story by making *conscious* the threads from which we derive our sense of meaning. I learned about cultural baskets in a deeply personal way, a high-desert wilderness retreat in native tradition, sleeping under a blanket of stars breathtaking beyond compare, waking to the howl of a coyote at dawn, and to sunrise that slowly painted the canyon walls with a soft red glow. As I sat quietly one morning near the remains of the previous night's campfire, warmed by the sun now piercing the desert's cold morning air, a teenager in the group walked quietly toward the fire pit and sat at its edge. Without a sound, yet with clear intention, he gathered twigs of sagebrush, bits of straw, a few bark peelings, and formed them into a ball, which he cradled in the palm of his hand. He then coaxed a single ember from the coals of last night's fire into the ball and blew on it lightly until smoke, then a spark, appeared. As he deftly set the glowing ball into the fire pit, we watched together; a fire was burning. It took perhaps fifteen minutes;

done in silence, in peace, with reverence and love. Yet it loudly declared his intention, belief in self, trust in the unknown, and deep connection with the land—no doubt threads of *his* cultural basket. And in that moment, of my basket, too.

An Invitation: Everything you think, say and do profoundly affects your life as well as the lives of others. You *choose* the energy (attitude, awareness, attention, acceptance, action) you put into life, then receive according to what you put in. What's possible in life comes wholly from your way of seeing; the more clarity and perspective defining your view, the more possibility you have. We're all storytellers; we create, tell and live stories. Our stories *create* our reality. How might you change your life's path simply by changing the story you tell? Think a moment; what *is* the story you tell? How does it compare to the story you live? How do choices you make affect *your* life? Lives of others? How would life be different if you lived from the knowing that all life is connected and that all you think, say and do affects everything else? Do you gratefully honor the gift that life is?

Practice: *An attitude of gratitude.* Although few of us may be able to comprehend how connectedness and wholeness truly work, we can imagine and appreciate being part of a far bigger world than the world we see each day. One way to experience gratitude and to explore connectedness in your life is to keep a "gratitude journal," noting each evening three things for which you are grateful that day. These need not be big; they might include noticing the smell of flowers, your own health, a call from a friend, how someone said "thank you" or just smiled. As you sit quietly and reflect each day, imagine that everything you believe, think, say and do ripples throughout the universe. *See* ripples of your thoughts and words spread in all directions, touching everything in their path. Is this not the power ascribed to envisioning, to prayer, to affirmation? We may never truly know how many lives we touch, or how we impact others, yet by imagining, we can see that when we choose love, possibility and joy, we create far different energy (and therefore potential) than we do when choosing fear, denial, judgment or resignation. Over the course of a year, this practice can shift your entire consciousness, enhancing acceptance and releasing judgment. It certainly did for me. When you focus on how much you already have, and are, anxiety and judgment fade, and you become your more authentic self. This perhaps trivial practice has amazing power to "connect you with life's connectedness," so you experience feeling more "at one" with all life.

AN INVITATION

Imagine if you *did* align your life context with nature's way. Envision yourself *becoming* your creative genius, rather than being someone else just to make a living. Envision how chaos can be an exciting opening to opportunity, rather than a threat to your safety and peace. Envision how life's natural feedback might guide your path, rather than a bunch of goals and measurement systems. Envision what it could be like if your senses of connectedness and community—with others, life, a higher power—acted as pure inspiration, rather than unattainable dream. How would you feel each day? Toward what would you direct the power of your conscious thought? You never *were* separate from nature anyway.

The felt experience of practice actually creates a new map to the territory of life, one that is uniquely your own—a reflection of *your* authentic self. As you walk the paths of *this* map, you feel at home. **You are**; it's *your* map. You'll likely also discover that the *map* does the work of changing you, so "you" don't have to. I've often noted that when you manage the context of your life (create the map), then details take care of themselves, naturally. Because the new map accurately represents **you**, it renders most choices either so obvious you don't have to agonize over them, or so inconsequential they don't have to be made at all. Little stuff no longer gets in the way of the big stuff.

Here's a story that serves as a metaphor for your power to *choose* context ... for your life, or even for the very next moment.

It's also a form of "proof" that there are always "many right answers." If you've ever been to Maui, or even if you haven't, you've likely heard of the celebrated drive to Hana. Hana is a small town on the less traveled side of the island, where a combination of trade winds and mountains brings a fair amount of rain. Lightly populated as a result, it seems life proceeds at a slower pace, almost as if clocks ran at a different speed. The popular drive to Hana is just over 30 miles long, but within those 30 miles, you'll negotiate some 160 hairpin turns. If, like many tourists, you set the *goal* of going to Hana, the trip could take perhaps two to three hours, leaving you with white knuckles, mild perspiration, a feeling of torture, and a real letdown on arrival—for there's just not much of anything there. If, on the other hand, like fewer tourists, you set out to *experience* the drive to Hana, what unfolds is far different: spectacular sea cliffs, verdant rainforest, splendid tropical flowers, ancient Hawaiian taro farms, breathtaking silence, the smell of moist earth, and a connection to the age-old pulse of life itself. If your only objective was to get to Hana, you miss all this in the midst of the torture of the drive.

Whether it's Hana, or life, the experience of getting there offers far more fulfillment and joy than the destination itself. To focus on the destination (or the answer) beforehand seems to preclude enjoyment and experience of the journey itself. And to complete the metaphor, it's the same road, no matter which experience you choose!

Such are the extremes in life context we experience, from unconscious at one end, to openness toward ever-expanding views of "life's truths" at the other. Deepak Chopra once offered a model of slow shifts in worldview, suggesting a parallel to shifts we, too, must make to grow into our own potential.

- In the past, *classical* science taught us to see our *lives* the way it sees the *world*: a place of linear action, predictability, repeatability, cause-and-effect, driven by mechanistic processes, largely devoid of inherent meaning—an objective world of *things*. This has been the "prevailing wisdom" for about 400 years, since the time of Galileo. This worldview has given rise to our "know more, try harder" culture, relying on linear, mechanistic thinking, planning outcomes ahead of time (goals) and proving everything we do. No wonder we feel lost.

- About 100 years ago, *quantum* science emerged, confounding classical science with nearly a complete breakdown in our view. Quantum science sees an interconnected web of possibility, where time and space are no longer constraints, where "effects" can happen without apparent "causes"—a world of *energy*. A world of "many right answers" driven only by our creative genius awaits us for the taking, or the believing. Yet we hold tightly (unconsciously) to classical ways, shunning as false the "inconvenient truth" of a world we can't fully understand.

- Even more recently, *emerging* science opens to a still larger view—that we *bring our world into being* through intention, perspective and perception, how we see and think, thereby *creating* life anew each moment—a subjective world of *consciousness*.

Living "*In Nature's Image*" brings these three views together, as one. Each is "true and valid" at its own level of consciousness. These views are neither separate nor in conflict; each one lives *inside* the next. The expansion of consciousness exposes larger and larger frameworks of truth. As awareness expands, possibility fills the space provided, so that larger, even more inclusive views of life may emerge. Not surprisingly, this is the only world *nature* has ever known.

[The next pages summarize nature's principles presented earlier—a "field guide to the field guide," as it were.]

IN NATURE'S IMAGE: AN ARCHETYPAL MODEL FOR LIFE DESIGN

In our desire to live with greater meaning and joy, we might simply look to nature for guidance. The ways of the universe, from spiral galaxies to delicate snowflakes to exquisite orchids to majestic polar bears, offer a natural model for living authentically and sustainably. If we were to design our lives *in nature's image*, we might "*re-member*" ourselves, and recall what nature teaches: to *create* with intention, *live* with awareness, *act* with courage, *relate* with reverence. "The way it is" in nature is an archetype for our deepest longing:

 **Creativity:** The entire universe is sustained by a singular energy—the *process of creative expression*, each element expressing its innate essence. This suggests that life isn't a *destination* or result to be attained, but rather a *journey* to be experienced. The creative process is the wellspring from which all possibility unfolds, energy that drives meaningful lives and thriving workplaces. *What if you could design your entire life around that deep personal truth to which you are continually drawn?*

Opportunism: Against a backdrop of continual change, life seizes the uncertainty in each moment, propagating itself in all directions, the essence of creative spirit. We therefore create our path in life by walking it, not by having it laid out ahead of time. Our  most powerful tools, then, are *patience*, to wait for openings; *awareness*, to notice when they occur; *acceptance*, that life will unfold so as to serve us; and *trust*, in our own innate essence. *What if you could view life's inherent uncertainty as an opportunity for your creative genius, rather than as a threat to your safety?*

Self-Organization: Life responds to *feedback*, an inherent attribute of all living systems, information within a system that guides its next steps. It's how creativity and opportunity unite to produce order from chaos, naturally. A personal culture of listening, inquiry and reflection offers a far more effective strategy for creating order than one based in command and control. *What if you could listen to, and implicitly trust, the clarity of your inner truth and your own experience to guide your next steps?*

Simultaneity: In nature, all possibility exists in each moment, "many right answers." Choosing one answer ahead of time, as with a goal, *limits* possibility, for it renders all others invisible from the start. You *create* more simply by learning to *see* more. In this  sense, there is no independent reality; reality is a natural consequence of how you look at life. *What if you could dramatically expand the edges of your current perception, allowing your creative energy to fill the open space?*

Rhythm: Underneath its surface chaos, life is incomprehensible order. Life's natural patterns offer far more meaning than the events comprising them. Birth and death; abundance and dearth; quiet space between. Without one, there is no other. Without emptiness, there is no room for new creation. Cycles are nature's way to renew and refresh. *What if you could graciously accept life's ups and downs, living more deeply in "the space between," opening without judgment to lessons of both the peaks and valleys?*

Energy: The unifying force in the universe is energy. Time and space are simply by-products of how energy manifests. Energy goes only into sustaining the process of creation—a process of elegant simplicity

with manifestations that are miraculously complex and diverse. *How do you use your energy, to create a life you'd love or to fight the one you've got? What if your awareness were so keen that you could devote energy only to what matters most ... your creative essence?*

Community: Survival and sustainability favor cooperation and collaboration, through the creation of adaptive and resilient systems of order—from galaxies to ecosystems to organisms to atoms—communities built around a common thread. Everything occurs "in relationship." Shared visions create energy that reinforces the essence of both individual and collective. *What if your connection with others could create a "spiral of possibility" around you, bringing out the best in yourself and in others?*

Connectedness: Everything in the universe is inextricably connected to everything else. Nothing survives as a fragment. We are united by the original energy of creation. The entire universe, therefore, is contained in every piece, no matter how small—as in a  hologram. Extracting pieces from their context under the guise of getting to know them has robbed life of its wholeness, and therefore its source of meaning. *What if you knew that how you see, think, speak and act has a profound effect, not only on your life, but on the lives of everything and everyone else, too?*

For over 400 years, *classical science* taught us to see *life* the way it sees the *world*: a place of predictability, repeatability, cause-and-effect, driven by mechanistic linear processes—an objective world of **things**. *Quantum science* sees a world of potential: an interconnected web of possibility, where time and space are no longer constraints—a world of **energy**. We are now opening to a still *larger view*: we *bring our world into being* through our intention, perspective and perception, *creating* life's experience in each moment—a subjective world of ***consciousness***. Science has its place, but as a worldview, it has become a life-limiting constraint to the joy and meaning we long for. The map is in front of us. Can we listen? Can we hear?

Chapter 6

Authentic Presence

Personal Responsibility

"It is no use walking anywhere to preach unless
our walking is our preaching."

– St. Francis of Assisi

INTRODUCTION

Imagine what it would be like if you were living the life of your dreams, every day, being wildly *creative and productive*, bringing your unique gifts to the world, with resilience, balance and meaning, regardless of life's circumstances. You can.

Imagine what it would be like if you could draw your energy from the fire burning inside you, your authentic truth, and no longer needed to seek that energy from others or the external world. You can.

Imagine what it would be like if you could choose your next steps, with confidence and grace, from the natural feedback life offered you, not from a fixed agenda, plan or goals, just by being your truth. You can.

This chapter is entitled **Personal Responsibility**. Its intent is to help you connect deeply with the power of your own consciousness, learning to be aware of, and take responsibility for, your thoughts, in each moment. One of many pathways to living authentically, this focuses most directly on the workings of your mind, both conscious and unconscious, and your growing *awareness* of your thinking as fuel to guide your journey to authenticity. As with other pathways, this assumes you have completed Part I of the Living Authentically program beforehand. And as is true for the others, this path leads you to personal experience of your inner truth, and consequently, self-trust.

I drew a Zen card recently labeled "Right Thought." It read, *"You are what you think. Think it today, become it tomorrow. Nothing can help you or hurt you as much as the thoughts you carry in your head."* So, I began to notice the thoughts running through my head. There's never a shortage: gratitude, worry, wonder, judgment. What thoughts do you carry in *your* head? Do you take the time to look ... as an observer, rather than as a participant alone?

As prone to habit as we are, we're generally unaware, at a conscious level, of thoughts that occupy our minds, largely because they've been in there so long they've just taken up residence. If forced to look, our perspective might even be this: "My mind is full … with thoughts; they must therefore be *my* thoughts; so I must therefore be thinking." Although we're generally too busy to consider deeper reflection, there's a problem with this quick response. Chances are that the thoughts in your head—ones you think you're thinking—belong to someone else; moreover, "you" aren't thinking them; the unconscious is "doing it for you."

By assuming this thinking is our own, and that we're doing it consciously, we come to rely on it, now *unconsciously* of course, to create the happiness we're working so hard to achieve. But our happiness doesn't live in someone else's thinking; nor does it live in our habituated, unconscious response. Although it's common to view happiness as something we experience when events outside us "make us happy," happiness in fact is a choice, the result of *conscious* thoughts; we choose to be happy by learning to see and think in new ways. Yet the home of such thinking, the conscious mind, is the one place we haven't developed enough so we can evoke our innate power to manifest a life we love. Thusly deceived, we wonder why life is difficult.

Habituated thinking is elusive, simply because we rarely notice aspects of ourselves that we've relegated to the unconscious. Yet herein lies the key to discovering the authentic self. By consciously examining our "prevailing thought frameworks," we make the unconscious conscious—which is key to changing it. By way of example, here are a few common frameworks of thought we unconsciously adopt. Once adopted, we tend to "become" them, as if we *had* chosen consciously. Step back from your "thinking" for a moment and see what these perspectives might teach you, about yourself, or about others in your life.

> **Science** is intended to help us explain what can be known rationally. As a viewpoint, it posits this: "I

must be able to separate a thing from its environment, measure it, repeat it, predict it and control it; then I know it's true." Humanness *isn't* these things, but that doesn't seem to stop us from seeing ourselves, and life, in such mechanistic terms.

Religion is intended to help us make sense of what *can't* be known rationally. It shows up as a *range* of viewpoints. At one end, "I have devoted my faith to what is written; I need not look further." At the other, "I have personal faith in what I can't know for sure, and here I find comfort and strength in a chaotic world."

Being "right" is a defensive strategy, adopted to protect a weak sense of self. As a viewpoint, it declares, "I'm always certain. I'm certain I'm *right*. I'll prove it by showing you that you're *wrong*."

Victimness is also a defensive strategy, blaming others for what's seen as hopeless. As a viewpoint, it cries, "I'm always certain, too. I'm certain I'm *wrong*. I'll prove it by showing how bad my life is, and how 'they' made it so."

Tribalism is home of "pretend thinking." As a viewpoint, it claims: "I don't have enough courage to think for myself so I'll adopt the ideas of others, then defend them as if I had experienced it all personally."

These are all just viewpoints. They're made up only of thoughts. All are developed by others, even if the other is your bruised ego. None have *independent truth of their own ... beyond what you give them*. Each viewpoint may have its role, but to adopt one in place of your own thinking or personal truth is probably not a valid choice. When you live through the thinking of *others* (science, religion, politics, media, group-think, personal history), well-intended or not, you abdicate responsibility for *your own* thinking, consciously or not. All you're left with is the futile chore of justifying or defending your "opinions."

The alternative, as this chapter explores, is to become a student of your thinking, perhaps choosing **curiosity** as your prevailing life viewpoint, thereby allowing your *awareness* and *personal presence* to guide your steps—consciously. Claiming full responsibility for your thoughts is an opening to your self-trust and authenticity.

Navigating the often-rocky pathways in my own life, as well as helping others with theirs, I've found that what lies at the heart of our struggles, challenges, stress and lack of meaning, along with the adopted viewpoints that arise from them, is an unconscious obsession with, or fear of, **uncertainty**. It's everywhere: hurricanes, earthquakes, disease, relationships, jobs, a truck around the next curve, every aspect of life. Intellectually, we accept this is true, but the fact is that we hate it. We like **knowing** things much better. It's a basic human need to feel safe, but we somehow equate "knowing more" with *certainty*. We then equate certainty with *safety*. But to build a thought framework for life on such a flimsy defense leaves us *less* safe, *less* certain, *less* secure. We can't defend ourselves against unknowns because we don't know what they are! Yet we sure lose energy trying.

Our world is far too complex for us to know everything. I'm not talking here about things we *can* know but just *don't*—like the distance to Mars, the population of Fiji, or names of the state capitals. I'm talking here about the challenging issues of our time—such as how to sustainably steward our planet and its resources; ethical implications of artificial intelligence and the internet; how to ensure a well-educated and healthy citizenship; how to keep our homes, communities and world safe places to live. These issues are insanely complex; they affect every aspect of our world: science, politics, economics, ethics, law, etc. None of these can be resolved into "one right answer," because their complexity defies the level of knowingness that could lead to one answer. So there's simply no way we can make choices for our lives in 100% confidence. And it bothers us no end to deal with this.

So how do we cope? Often, we **pretend**. Because we've been taught to be *afraid of not knowing*, we pretend we *do* know. Or we pretend we don't care. It's pure delusion, yet every day we consistently deny "not knowing," which admittedly can be deeply unsettling, and adopt what amounts to nothing more than *opinions*. Our framework of "truth" can't possibly be large enough to do better. But ... we then proceed to *call* them facts, which we in turn feel obligated to defend, sometimes violently, against the "facts" of others, as they're threats to our delusion. We find comfort anyway, telling ourselves that a satisfying un-truth is better than an un-satisfying, incomplete truth. The thinking goes: "at least I can be sure of my opinions." Yet while we do so, *questioning* stops; *thinking* stops; and *learning* stops. In addition, it's all just exhausting. As chapter 2 explored in some detail, this adopted thinking and the adopted self that emerges from it creates a serious obstacle to authentic living. Yet we're unaware it's happening. This turns out to be an adaptive strategy with disastrous consequences.

An analogy: in nature, there's a phenomenon called "fight or flight." It's a first-stage response to stress in the environment, nature's way to cope with changes that happen too quickly to allow for evolutionary adaptation. A well-known example is the lemming, a small Arctic rodent. When lemming populations grow too rapidly, as they do when conditions are favorable, they get stressed and resort to fleeing—en masse. The highly misrepresented story is that lemmings commit suicide by jumping off cliffs—en masse. The less dramatic, yet truthful, story is that, fleeing—en masse, a lot of lemmings reach the edge of a cliff, and before the one in front can say, "uh-oh," the one in the rear pushes him over. And so on. Had the original researcher been a more careful observer, he'd have noticed the detail. The point: in times of stress, "thinking," to the extent lemmings "think," is hijacked by instinct.

I suspect the parallel with human response is both clear and valid. Our world is becoming more unpredictable, uncertain and complex, at a rate greater than we can meaningfully adapt. *We* experience that as stress, too. Yet we're endowed with a capacity lemmings don't have—*conscious awareness of our thoughts*. We can be *aware* of our environment, *aware* of our stress, and *free* to make new choices, a highly-advanced form of response. Yet we don't often use this capacity. Why not? Have we allowed "fight or flight" to hijack **our** conscious thought, too?

~~~

The only missing ingredient in living authentically is consciousness.

~~~

What's the path forward? Perhaps counterintuitive, the best way to learn about your consciousness is to learn how your *un*consciousness has kept you from it. Intellectually you know your life holds potential greater than you've experienced. But *knowing* that doesn't change you. Why? Because the unconscious holds power over you, until you notice it for what it is—more the Wizard of Oz than the real deal.

Stop for a moment and see if you discover, through quiet personal reflection, some of the bad lessons that may be lodged today in your unconscious mind as truth. These lessons hold you back. Here are a few examples. (See chapter 2 for more on this.) How do these compare to your list?

- I'm not good enough
- What others think of me matters, even defines who I am
- I can't make a living doing what I love
- Force and control get more done better than calm presence
- The answers to life and happiness live in the external world, where I must fight my way to finding them and making them happen
- Life is supposed to be difficult

Now stop for a few more moments of reflection. Think of statements you would *like* to be true for you, but today are not. Here's a sample of ideas I commonly hear:

- I know myself; self-trust powers my life, not the opinions of others

- I treat others, and myself, the same way—with respect and reverence, whether I agree with them or not

- I have a strong sense of my gifts, and bring them to the world

- I design my life, and my days, around the expression of my inner truth, and around my own well-being, not the demands of others

- I choose a personal culture of learning; every situation is a teacher

- Personal authenticity means far more to me than social acceptance

- I don't worry about life's details; when I choose the framework in which details happen, they take care of themselves

- I may live inside life's circumstances, but *I* am not those circumstances; I won't give them the power to ruin my day

- Although my past may have brought me to where and who I am, it won't take me where I want to go; trusting my innate essence will

- I believe there are many right answers to every challenge

- My life represents unlimited possibility; the same is true for others

- I don't choose an outcome or agenda beforehand; I have no need to control events or others; I trust my experience to show me the way

Read the list again, this time imagining yourself *being* the person each statement describes. What would life be like for you if these statements were true for you? Just imagine ... for now.

These ideas are part of your authentic self. That's the "self" of innate potential, the self-described in Chapter 1. We all come into this world as trusting, innocent, collaborative, creative beings. Then we learn we're not. Are you filled with the curiosity, wonder, freedom and creativity you experienced as a child? Where did they go? They're still there, just hidden—under a pile of bad lessons and unexamined assumptions about how you, and life, are supposed to work. While you may unconsciously blame "life" for your stress and anxiety, there's no stress or anxiety generated in being yourself. What now?

We might start by recognizing that life's chaos, complexity and uncertainty don't ask for our judgments, our opinions, or for us to "fix" them. They ask us to *learn* from them, then respond, using our creative genius. We don't need to know everything. (Good thing, because we can't.) The obstacle: admitting this.

What if we could adopt "a culture of not knowing" as an opening to curiosity and understanding—about ourselves, others, life, our planet, and even the cosmos? If we could stop to inquire within, we might notice the *implications* of our defensiveness, and then begin to see and think in new ways. Perhaps, as Wendell Berry suggests, we need "a language of ignorance," one not oriented toward blame, shame or guilt, but rather toward acceptance, openness and learning. What if we could set out to *learn* about all we *think* we know, but don't: secrets of the universe, the magic of consciousness, the mystery life is, the depths of our humanness, how to live together on this planet peacefully and sustainably? We'd never be "done" learning, yet we'd move beyond the delusion of pretending, the illusion of knowing, and find home in curiosity instead.

A path of authenticity involves learning to live with two conflicting ways of seeing without making one of them wrong.

You come to this "wisdom of not knowing" through awareness and acceptance. As you *get to know your fears*, instead of hiding or fighting them, you discover the thinking that created them, and the fears fall away. You're left with truth—your own. Truth doesn't need proof; it just "is." As you see a bigger world, you become part of a bigger world. You experience *resonance*—an energy match between your truth and the potential that world holds for your creative genius. Because this energy is everywhere, it's available to everyone. Few experience it, simply because it invites deeper contemplation and self-awareness than most can tolerate.

With courage to engage in deeper inquiry, you begin to see life's wholeness rather than the separateness you may have believed courtesy of voices in your head. You soon realize you're not "separate" at all, but part of something much bigger; and that your former, perhaps fear-based, viewpoint of believing small serves neither you nor the world. When you realize you *belong here*, you feel resilient and confident, despite society's attempt to steer you onto a narrower path. This awareness is powerful fuel for self-trust, resilience and truth—a life of purpose and intention. In addition, you see that living this way is a choice, a choice available to you in each moment.

Living authentically is, at its heart, about self-trust. As you learn to trust yourself (your truth, uniqueness, consciousness, personal presence), you *become* authentic. That is a very different process than trying to *make* yourself be authentic. And you become authentic through a process of personal discovery—*getting to know* the "you" underneath all the assumptions and beliefs "you" may have unconsciously become over years of lack of awareness.

This is *context* work—it's about the framework of thinking surrounding the *content* of your life. As a society, we're pretty obsessed with content—believing we must manage all life's details, control the outcomes of our efforts, and know where we're headed in each moment. We honestly believe that the details *are* life. Not only is this pursuit futile, as we can never control it all, but in our obsession to make it happen anyway, we miss altogether the fact that these details are a direct result of the consciousness framework surrounding them. We actually *created* the details by virtue of the thinking (or lack of it) we've used to drive our lives—a *context* that is unconscious and life-constricting instead of consciously-chosen and possibility-filled, one that has distorted our view of the details to the point that we've misidentified them as the enemy. You change your life by changing the way you see and think about it—to a way that aligns with your emerging sense of inner truth and authentic self. As you learn to devote your energy to being aware of, and purposefully choosing, the *context* of your life, the *content* of your life will flow with ease and grace—all on its own, naturally.

~~~

"Draw a different frame around the same set of circumstances and new pathways come into view. Find the right framework and extraordinary accomplishment becomes an everyday experience."
– Ben and Roz Zander, in <u>The Art of Possibility</u>

~~~

BECOMING YOUR AUTHENTIC SELF: FIVE PHASES

You are unique; your truth is uniquely your own. The journey to discover and live it, however, leads down a common path—a path made up of growing conscious awareness, personal clarity, release of judgment, and discarding old lessons. The path is framed by your consciousness, how your life has influenced you. With practices offering *perspective and clarity on the life story of your thinking*, you open yourself, easily and naturally, to the authentic *you* underneath. You therefore don't *do* each step in the path, but *become* it—through **felt experience** of its truth. Knowing doesn't change you; felt experience of knowing does.

Here's a summary of the path; the pages that follow explore the details.

I. Perception. (It Is) Gain complete clarity and acceptance that "the way it is" today just *is*. Release *all* judgment; it just **is**. This is true of every part of your life, all that happens to you, even who you believe you are. It just **is**. This doesn't mean you *like* the way it is, but that you *see* it all *as* it is. Truth is separate from your opinion about it.

II. Perspective. (It's Mine) Gain complete clarity and acceptance that "the way it is" is a **natural consequence** of your *thinking*. What you experience as reality isn't "truth," but an "interpretation of truth," the result of old lessons, beliefs and experiences. Interpretation is the *life story of your **thinking**.* You are the causal factor in your reality.

III. Possibility. (It Could Be) Create in your mind, then continually replay to yourself, a vivid, powerful vision of you living your unique truth. You can do this for a lifetime, a job, a project, a conversation, or being a specific competency you desire. Unlike goals, which *limit* possibility, visions are expansive; they *create* possibility.

IV. Action. *(I Am)* Nurture *conditions* for your vision to manifest. Take one action step into your truth each day. Let go of how it turns out; just focus on ***being*** it. With each step, listen for ***feedback***, a natural information flow in every living system that guides the system's next steps. Your truth manifests through action and feedback, not through goals.

V. Regeneration. *(I Become)* Sustain your vision and truth for a lifetime by adopting personal practices in three areas of life: (1) extreme self-care, (2) trusting your inner truth to guide your life, (3) connecting deeply with yourself, nature, higher power, community of support. Practices allow you to become your true self, to trust yourself fully. You become what you practice.

Before leading you onto the path to your authentic self, I offer what may well be a repetitive message. At the same time, it's a message that can either make or break your journey. Experience has taught me that it's therefore worth repeating.

You know by now that the major obstacle to discovering your true self is a host of old lessons and beliefs, lodged in your unconscious mind, often so deeply you can't imagine they're false. And since you've not stopped to question them, you're unlikely to even know they're there. Two such beliefs are common sources of trouble, failure or resignation, despite the fact that we're often unaware of, or even deny, their impact.

As a society, it seems we've become rather obsessed with two ideas: (1) that "taking immediate action" is always beneficial, and (2) that "experiencing immediate results" is not only possible and desirable, but is also a measure of success. So ingrained as they are in our minds, we can't imagine a world where results occur over time frames longer than our patience allows us to tolerate. So we spring into action too soon, unaware that our action is guided by those same old thoughts we're working so hard to release. We thereby miss altogether the opportunity to bring the true power of our consciousness to bear on life's possibility. As noted earlier, life in this world is more like tending a garden; you nurture conditions for great potential, but the "results" happen in response to your nurturing, not your force.

To conduct the personal inquiry needed to discover, then live, your true self, you'll need to hold these two tendencies in abeyance. In fact, you need to kill them altogether. Paving this path for the steps that follow is detailed in "The Basics" portions of the Living Authentically program. If you've internalized practices offered there, you're ready to continue. If you haven't, then you'll unconsciously be using the same thinking that has **kept** you from your authentic self all these years in your effort to **find** that authentic self. It won't work. He or she doesn't live where that thinking takes you. It's another example of trying to change from the outside in. Lasting change manifests from the inside out.

Let's set out to explore the territory of your consciousness.

~~~

Living a story *about life isn't the same as living* life.

~~~

I: PERCEPTION—*IT IS*

"In the attitude of silence the soul finds the path in a clearer light, and what is elusive and deceptive resolves itself into crystal clearness. Our life is a long and arduous quest after Truth."
– Mahatma Gandhi

~~~ Accept: *"The way it is" … just is."* ~~~

Introduction: The first phase in the journey to your authentic self is to gain complete clarity and non-judgmental acceptance that "the way it is" today just *is*. The work here is to learn to see yourself, others, situations, the world, even life itself with both clarity and objectivity, thereby releasing all judgment. "The way it is" just *is*. To *accept* the way it is doesn't mean you *agree* with, or *like*, the way it is, but that your *opinion* about life isn't part of your *reaction* to life … because your opinion has no impact. (Your dislike of rain never changed the weather.) Separating "the way it is" from your *judgment* of it opens up space for possibility to rush in. Acceptance asks not for your judgment, but for your creative genius. No matter the situation, the only question that matters is, "What's possible now?"

The Potential: If you're like most, you live more of an *interpretation* of life than "life," simply by seeing everything through a lens of judgment. Learning to see beyond this judgment, however, you begin to realize how much of your energy goes into defending your opinion about how things *should be* instead of creating possibility from what's directly in front of you. You also experience clear, objective thinking, perhaps for the first time. Awareness gained through this shift in perspective creates more energy for true change than any amount of trying could ever do. Step into "what *could* be." There's a maxim attributed to Arthur Ashe that offers three pieces of advice: "*Start where you are; use what you have; do what you can.*" Or … you can't start someplace you're not; you can't begin with what you think you *should* have; you can't do what you can't do. *It is what it is.* Living this way offers freedom to be and do your best.

The Obstacle: Early lessons and life experience generally taught us to *judge* "the way it is," not accept it. We learned to see what's *wrong* or what *should be* rather than what's *possible* or what *is.* Lack of awareness this is *happening* keeps you from noticing; lack of acceptance that it's *true* keeps you from finding your truth. You just can't use judgment to create a life free of it. Worse, because it's all unconscious, you may miss altogether the fact that the stress and hostility you experience in life are of your own creation, a "natural" result of lack of acceptance. This keeps your world small—a defense mechanism for the scary place you've created in your mind. In defense, you spend your energy trying to control life's outcomes. It doesn't work. We often have no clue what we really want, yet at the same time, we're angry we don't have it.

The Path Beyond: Learning to see and accept things as they are is huge work for most people, ingrained as old lessons and beliefs have become ... and the life strategies they've spawned. It's all become unconscious background, often to the point that you may find even this idea a stretch. *Discovering* this backdrop of judgment, however, opens you to how old assumptions have inhibited your sense of possibility by clouding your perception. The "simple" act of getting to know these judgments allows you to release their stories ... and along with them, the limiting habits they generate. By so doing, you might trade a culture of judgment for a culture of curiosity instead. Curiosity and wonder are innate; you may know them only as voices in your head, voices which, although lost in the din of all the others, remind you tomorrow is a place of limitless potential, a world not yet invented, a world willing to shape itself to match the loftiest thoughts you hold. When you release what you think "should be," you hear, and can then honor, them. But how?

How do you know where you're *not* accepting what is? How do you know where you're *not* thinking with clarity and objectivity? Better, how do you know you *are*? You *notice.* With practices suggested below, you see your perception in action. You learn to see where perception is clouded, how you judge, how you live from what you think should be rather than from what is.

You see the impact of your judgment. It shows up as emotion. Most emotions come from thoughts, generally thoughts about failing to accept "what is." As soon as you experience such a feeling, you unconsciously react ... by trying to change things. Most instances of stress, anger, resentment, guilt, anxiety, fear or dread come from an often-hidden belief that "the way it is" isn't ok—with you, *and* that you need to change it. Self-reflective practices open the window to this awareness. And when you can see this mechanism at work, you stop doing it. You stop "justifying" your emotion and begin learning from it. You need only *notice* your thinking at work for this shift to materialize. Imagine the energy you'd free up for more worthwhile pursuits if you didn't have to use it judging and controlling life.

And ... as judgment falls away, you notice that you now respond to ideas, events, situations, other people, life and even yourself, with "isn't that curious" instead. The stress, anger, resentment, guilt, anxiety, fear or dread that once defined your life are gone.

Example: I recall an idea from the book, <u>The Shack</u>, by William Young, noting the difference between **expectation**, that something must happen in a certain way, and **expectancy**, that anything is possible. One seems to justify resentment and revengefulness because things don't often go as we'd like, while the other fills us with hope and curiosity over what the next moment may hold. The difference between them? *Judgment.* Here are a few questions that can bridge the gap. What if you could learn to see the world (and hey, maybe even yourself) with **curiosity** instead of **judgment**? What if you didn't have your mind already made up? What if you were willing to have life's experience *change* you? What if you actually had to think *forward,* to understand the implications of opinions you hold strongly? What if you actually had to think *backward*, to understand the thought process that brought you to those opinions in the first place? Would you still think as you do? Unlike judgment-based thinking, curiosity-based thinking leads to relatedness and compassion for others and self, as well as to self-acceptance and learning. It already sounds peaceful, even before trying it!

My Story: I tire even from the recollection ... that everything in my life had to go the way I was taught it should go, and the arrogant, misguided belief I could make it happen that way. I had been *taught* that. I know now that it was not part of the authentic *me*. For most of my childhood, however, I stressed over why it had to be that way. I never questioned that it didn't. I note now, that if I *had* questioned it, my stress would have waned. So, armed with that "lesson," I then spent most of my adult life living in judgment of, and therefore trying to control, everything ... to the detriment of professional and personal relationships, my effectiveness, and, clearly, my authentic self. No wonder I was angry, resentful and stressed. And no wonder I didn't know why. My entire 40-year career in high tech was, in hindsight, nothing more than a futile, yet unconscious, attempt to live out life-constricting lessons of the 20 years preceding it. Making life happen, by living "the world according to my dad"—a world of judgment, command-and-control, and selfishness—my perception was so clouded and my perspective so narrow that I didn't even stop to wonder if there could be more to life. I ate well, but I was starving. It took the loss, in a single year, of all I'd been *taught* to work a lifetime for—job, professional reputation, marriage, home, and retirement account—for me to even notice this was happening. I recall waking up mornings wondering who I was; all I *thought* defined me was gone—a painful opening to the need for a shift in perception.

The Practice: Years of unconsciously following old lessons often leave us obsessed with instant action and instant results. We think it's who we are, what life is really about. As a result, we're impatient with personal inquiry, quiet time, reflection, etc. Instead, we act immediately, often without thinking, (or, without conscious, clear and objective thinking), then fixing later whatever we get wrong. We even believe this is productive. This attempt to change life *from the outside in* is futile. Change happens *from the inside out*. Change also happens, not by fixing, but by un-doing what created the obstacles in the first place, which just happens to be your thinking! A consciousness of acceptance doesn't happen overnight; it could take a year, ingrained as old thoughts are. The desire to rush can inhibit your path to the authentic you.

A practice of personal silence is the pathway to this awareness, and to consequent acceptance of what is. Silence brings your awareness to the *present* moment. That's the moment you usually miss while trying to make the *next* moment turn out your way instead. Silence creates space for new opportunities to manifest, potential that is always there, but that goes by unnoticed when life is full of noise and overwhelm. New opportunities show up in these gaps; if there are no gaps, there's no room for opportunity. The silence your mind hates is the silence your authentic inner self longs for. Sit quietly alone for 20 to 30 minutes each day. Relax your body; take a few deep breaths. Breathe purposefully; listen. Just be present; there's no right or wrong. Thoughts may continually arise, often in the form of inner voices, things to do, fears, etc. View them as clouds; watch as they pass by. "It just is what it is."

As you gain comfort with silence (you will) you might now frame your silence with a few big questions, questions that help expose judgment or lack of acceptance in your consciousness. Ask yourself:

- What's my "relationship" with my thoughts? When I think—about myself, another person, a situation, work or life—does the thought *flow through me*, or do I hold onto it, judging it or trying to change it?

- For those I hold onto, can I notice "how" I hold on ... maybe assigning them a label—"like/dislike" or "agree/disagree" or "right/wrong?"

- What do the thoughts I *hold onto* have in common with each other?

- What do thoughts that *flow through* have in common with each other?

- How do these two answers differ?

- What do I gain or lose by virtue of the *way* I relate to my thoughts? "Be with this question" a while, so as to explore it more deeply.
- What do I long for in life?
- Where does my curiosity lead me now, if I allow it?

II: PERSPECTIVE—*IT'S MINE*

"When you change the way you look at things,
the things you look at change."
– Wayne Dyer

~~~ **Understand***: Your thinking created "the way it is."* ~~~

Introduction: The next phase in the journey to your authentic self asks you to dig more deeply into "what is," and to now gain complete clarity and non-judgmental acceptance that "the way it is" is a **natural consequence** of your *thinking. You* are the causal factor in your reality. The work here is to gain acceptance of the direct relationship between your thinking and reality. Your experience of life is as it is because you have brought it into being with your thinking ... even if largely-unconscious.

The Potential: While it's common, because it's learned, to blame the external world for life's challenges, stress and struggle, the truth is that they are of your own creation—a direct, yet unconscious, result of how you learned to see and think. You know now that you learned to adopt the thinking of *others* as your own. As you discover *your* authentic thoughts, you're then free to think about life as a possibility, not as a problem. You're free to choose your thoughts. Nothing in yesterday's world suggests this is even possible, yet to claim 100% responsibility for your thoughts as the cause of your reality is perhaps the most freeing step you can make in life, simply because it leaves you 100% in control of the only thing in life you **can** control— your thinking. Seeing life as it truly is, you discover your true power to change it.

The Obstacle: By virtue of having learned to see others, life and the world as the cause of your struggles (i.e., blaming the wrong enemy), you've unknowingly abdicated responsibility for the true source of your challenge (and your potential) and how you've come to think about them. Old lessons taught you that life is difficult, that you have to control how life goes, that stress and anxiety are normal. If you *want* life to be tough, if you *want* to fight with life, or if you *want* to feel stress, it might work to keep this blame game alive. To me, bearing the burden of other people's thinking isn't worth that. Because you believe it's *your* thinking, however, you can't imagine that this not only caused the problem, but **is** the problem. You can't think 'outside the box' because your thinking *is* the box! Unaware the struggle is made up in your head, you believe you have no power to change it. How you use your consciousness is a choice (at least now that you know it is). Will you choose to honor your own thoughts, or is it still easier to pay the price of going along with the thinking of others?

The Path Beyond: Many dismiss as impossible the *idea* that thinking creates reality. Then there's what it implies—that you can change your life by changing your thinking. If that be your view, the journey stops here. If you've come this far, however, I suspect you're at least curious, if not open, to new ideas and ways. Let's face it, if old ways had been as effective as your old lessons told you they would be, you'd be happy, productive and at peace by now, right? Any chance old lessons and the thinking they spawned may be the culprit, not your skill or effort?

Focusing your energy on others denies you the experience of yourself, and of the present moment. Always looking to the external world, why would you see any potential in self-reflection? Yet if you made your thoughts conscious, you'd see your mind at work, including both how it constrains the potential you are *and* how it could manifest that potential as well. In denial, however, we live a *story* about life instead of life.

Adopted ways of thinking have led us to rely on a single prevailing strategy or competence for dealing with life. It's the same strategy we chose long ago to gain approval from others. *Using* that skill *well* defines the edges of our comfort zone, or life context; unconscious *over-reliance* on that skill keeps us from expanding it. By habituating what we're good at, we become blind to other choices, so we remain stuck.

Once we come to understand and accept our own role in the reality we experience, we open to the fact that in order to experience "the way it could be," we need to change the *thinking* that **created** "the way it is." And this is a "problem" fully in our control. No longer need we blame life, others, the world, or *ourselves*.

Example: We can often learn a lot about ourselves just by listening—to our internal stories, to the world around us, and specifically to nature. In nature, everything *belongs*. Nature just keeps creating, even in the face of adversity—responsible for everything, accepting everything, judging nothing. Here is a rather random, and perhaps fanciful, set of "observations on life," some from nature and some decidedly human, that may help to illuminate the idea of acceptance, and lack of it:

- Life on earth has been a 4.6-billion-year celebration of creativity. It seems life could be more meaningful if we joined instead of fought.

- Even if one side won today's "war of divisiveness," 49% are still angry, a world divided. What if we committed to possibility thinking, together, not a position-based search for that one right answer?

- Facebook won't be around in 100 years. Yet our concern for respect, dignity, integrity and privacy will live on. What truly matters here?

- "You cannot travel the path until you have become the path." Buddha

- Cockroaches have lived for 300 million years. They were here before dinosaurs, survived them all, and will likely survive us as a species. Why? They keep doing "what works," not fighting "what doesn't."

- Trees don't have to *try* to grow. Everything needed to become a tree is "hidden" in the seed.

- Accepting "what is" leads to wisdom; fighting it leads to judgment.

- The farther from earth you go, the fewer divisions you see. You don't have to go too far to see oneness, wholeness, lack of separateness.

- Seeing earth as "home" is part of a personal consciousness ... not a political position, nor a house in the country.

- Freedom is the absence of self-doubt.

- Mountains, trees, birds, waves and winds have seen this all. Might we listen to what they know? Might we learn?

- Possibility lies at the edge of your current perception.

- There's no competition for authenticity; no one can be a better you than you.

- Every original culture on this planet *lived* these ideas, without "needing proof." How much wisdom have we lost?

My Story: Back then, I thought nothing was wrong. Living and being as I'd learned was "so," I signed on to one of life's difficulties after another. My upbringing led me to a common "prevailing strategy" for approaching everything in life—getting things right. Taught I needed to do just that as a way to earn love, I complied, unaware I was living a lie. The world cooperated, however; business rewards those who are obsessed with working hard. My relationships, however, didn't like being "fixed." It all went reasonably well ... up to a point. And the point was when "fighting with life" left me *less* productive, *more* stressed, *less* happy, and very alone. I'd reached the edge of what worked, but didn't realize it. I was too busy trying to make it work. But slowly I learned that by *overdoing* what I thought was a great strategy, I'd limited the very potential I was determined to create. It took a few more years before I realized the cause was my thinking, not my level of skill or effort. My over-reliance on command-and-control had cost me. *Life* hadn't failed me; my *assumptions* about life had failed me. In a sad moment of self-realization, yet one that was to open huge doors, I came to see how instead of being driven to "get things right," I'd be far better served by *helping others* get it right, leading with compassion rather than pushing with brute force. Small shift; huge potential.

The Practice: Only by interrupting the incessant flow of unconscious voices you *think* is thinking will you get to know your truth. *Observing* your thoughts gives you a perspective you'd never get as a *participant* alone. You see your thinking at work, so you can discover the thoughts that are holding your life hostage. *Stop* what you're doing three or four times a day. During a few moments of quiet reflection, replay in your mind thoughts you've had since the last replay, as if a movie with you as its audience. **Listen** to what they tell you. Resist judging or trying to change them. Just notice. Again, an inquiry, not an overnight "task."

As you gain comfort observing your thoughts, getting to know them, building a relationship with them, and seeing how they are responsible for the course your life has taken, you might add a few questions to frame your inquiry. As thoughts run through your mind, focus on the ones that feel like "your truth," the ones to which you say, "Yes!" (Also notice those you reject, the ones to which you say, "No!") Ask yourself:

- Do I hold this truth as a result of deep personal inquiry? What *thinking* or *life experience* brought me here?

- Does my truth *invite/include/accept* everyone, without judgment or condition? Or does it shield me from others?

- For those thoughts I find myself rejecting as untrue, how did I come to accept them up until now? What changed?

- Can I discover where and how my most closely, yet unconsciously held truths have helped me get to where I am? Can I also discover how *over-reliance* on those same ideas has *limited* me from being myself? Can I see how my life has been a direct expression of my thinking, whether conscious or unconscious, effective or not?

- For what I *don't know* ... do I pretend I do? Do I retreat in fear? How do I relate to my not knowing? No need for judgment; just learning.

- What assumptions might I be making, perhaps without my conscious awareness, that serve to *support* a truth/thought/belief on one hand, yet at the same time *limit* me from seeing even larger truths?

- How might those who see the world differently from me answer these questions? How might they have arrived at "their" truth?

- If I could expand the edges of *my* thinking far enough to include *their* thinking, what *dialogue* might we then be able to share? How could more become possible as a result?

- Knowing I'm free to choose my thoughts, even my "prevailing life strategy," what thinking will best serve me, others, my life's potential, and the world? Am I willing to practice choosing that thinking?

III: Possibility—*It Could Be*

> *"And is it not a dream which none of you remember having dreamt that builded this city and fashioned all there is in it? Could you but see the tides of that breath you would cease to see all else, and if you could hear the whispering of the dream you would hear no other sound. The veil that clouds your eyes will be lifted by the hands that wove it."*
> – Kahlil Gibran, in *The Prophet*

~~~ Envision*: Imagine living a life you love.* ~~~

Introduction: The third phase of the journey to your true self invites you to "bring a new world into being." Your emerging acceptance, self-awareness and clarity open you to the innate, yet largely untapped, powers of consciousness and life potential that live inside you.

The Potential: As noted in Chapter 1, The Power of Human Potential, two amazing powers are innately your own. One is unique to you—your reason for being here, special gifts that are yours alone to bring to the world. The other makes us human—the power to manifest those gifts, using the power of consciousness. We're all familiar with the power of the mind to *describe*; it's how we live (planning, rationalizing, measuring, predicting, judging, doing.) You may be so entrenched in those powers, "trying to use them to control life," that you've lost awareness of the *imaginative* powers of the mind—to create, to manifest. That power is invoked through envisioning.

The Obstacle: Throughout life, we've learned to believe more in what we learned from others than in our own felt experience. We learned to trust others over ourselves; to rely on what we can see, touch and measure; to treat life as literal and linear, a world of five senses. Accepting this story as truth (which you might well have exposed in Phase II - Perspective), we often deny the unique *potential* we represent, as well as the power of our consciousness to manifest it. Believe it or not, like it or not, you even imagined *today* into being, even if only unconsciously. Today is a perfect reflection of the energy you put into the world. Your consciousness responded; it gave you just what you "asked" for. So, in perhaps a twisted kind of way, you've already proven the power of the mind to deliver what you "want." And in just the same way as you *unconsciously* adopted false beliefs long ago, you can *consciously* adopt new beliefs, and the thoughts they spawn, that serve your potential instead of being obstacles to it. In so doing, you manifest *those thoughts* with your thinking instead.

The Path Beyond: Tomorrow hasn't been invented yet. You are its inventor. The power of your consciousness offers fuel for new invention. Although you are probably far more used to *planning* tomorrow, maybe even *predicting* it, both planning and predicting are based on the notion that what happened yesterday defines what happens tomorrow. This is why your tomorrows may look alarmingly like yesterday. There's another path; it's called *envisioning*. Envisioning uses the mind's *imaginative* power, not its *rational* power. It begins with an open mind, a clean slate, and willingness to allow life to change you. "Struggles" are unnecessary when you envision, unless of course, you *want* them in your new life. Freed from the constraints of today's issues, you can listen to your inner truth, and allow ***it*** to imagine a new day into being. Imagining a future *creates* that future. It's how Walt Disney created the Magic Kingdom, how J. K. Rowling created Harry Potter. Envisioning is not about planning or predicting the future, but about giving your dreams energy, offering them space to manifest. By repeatedly imagining a future you love, you actually create a "memory of the future" for the unconscious mind, so as you take even one step into it (Phase IV), the unconscious mind (defender against all things unknown) recognizes this world as home, so it doesn't try to block you by telling you it's scary. A vision draws its power from uniting rational energy (what you love) with emotional energy (why it matters deeply to you) ... which creates *meaning*. Meaning evokes commitment; everything else evokes only compliance. Think of a *vision* as *a possibility to live into*. By contrast, the more common *goal* is *an expectation to live up to*. Visions inspire; goals constrain. Feel the difference? Repeatedly envisioning living your potential causes the mind to believe and behave as if it were already so.

Example: History offers myriad examples of visionaries. We may just see them as big thinkers, but their true power came from bringing their dreams to fruition, which they did through the power of consciousness. Disney clearly was one. JFK was another; no one had ever created such an image as a "man on the moon by 1970" as he did. His vision evoked the action to make it happen. Without that, stepping into the unknown may not have happened; it needed the power of the vision in order to create meaning. Martin Luther King "had a dream," an image that brought major change to civil rights. Polynesian voyagers, 3,000 years ago, discovered most of the islands in 10 million square miles of Pacific Ocean, by being crystal clear observers, and by keeping visions of their dreams, and their homeland, always in their mind. We know visionaries for the results they achieved; yet it's the process that created them that mattered most. Your greatest vision may not "rival" any of theirs, but comparison is meaningless; your truth, however, is not.

My Story: If you don't yet know your unique reason for being here, the exercise below can help. Here's how my experience of that exercise changed my life some 20 years ago. Reflecting on the various phases of my life, I discovered that the one thing they all had in common was that I was always asking big questions, questions to help me understand and see the bigger picture involved. No matter the circumstances, situation, people involved, stakes at risk, or emotions in the moment, I wanted to know *why*. A constant search for greater meaning has defined every part of my life—student, software guy, manager, spouse, parent, nature tour leader, Air Force officer, college professor, coach—I always asked big questions. This went over better in some circles than in others. Yet it was who I was. Discovering this "life theme" led me to coaching—helping others reframe their lives so more is possible. All of a sudden, my life made sense for the first time.

The Practice: Envisioning works for any aspect of your life and at any level—your whole life, a project, a job, a vacation, a conversation, even being a specific competency you desire. Envision living the full expression of your unique truth. A state of quiet reflection opens you to that truth. As you *feel* the emotional energy and meaning of the life you'd love, you can then mold it into a full-scale "movie" in your mind. Creating a bold image of a desirable future causes the mind to believe it **as if it were so**. Repeatedly replaying it in your mind cements it as "so." These practices hold phenomenal power.

1) Discover your personal truth. If you're not yet deeply connected with your unique truth (soul, authentic self, reason for being here), start here. Until you know what matters most, your energy goes unconsciously into upholding old beliefs of how life *should be*. You *feel* your true essence many times a day, pointing to your truth, asking you to listen. It wants to express itself through how you live. You discover it by *noticing!* This practice is a *life-long inquiry* into what matters to you. It creates a beacon lighting your life's path and fueling the journey. Daily at first, perhaps monthly after: sit quietly; name distinct *phases* of life. Possibilities include family, work, relationships, transitions. Some overlap is OK. For *each phase*, one at a time, ask: Who was I always being? What was I always drawn to? What did I do whether I gained approval or not? What did I wonder or imagine? Look for places in your *always* answers that ran against convention. A favorite from my school days: "I don't care about formulas; tell me *how it works* and I'll give *you* the formula." Review notes and see what you find *in common across phases*. As you discover who you can't *not* be/do, you find the piece of yourself that is so naturally *you* that you may have missed your own unique essence (soul, purpose), the "you" that got lost in all life's pressures to conform.

Your truth is a "pattern" deep inside you. You learn to recognize it as you would a friend's voice in a noisy room. With clarity and awareness, answers you struggle with today become obvious or inconsequential. After you get a sense of your true self, begin to listen to its message. Reflect quietly several times a day. See if you can identify instances in the present where your deepest longing (first part of this exercise) spoke to you. How did you respond in that moment? Did you hear it? Did you honor the message; did you deny or ignore it in favor of what was happening at the time?

2) Envisioning your future. In your imagination, create your future as a movie, with you as star. Imagine yourself living the life of your dreams, a life that evokes the heart, soul and spirit of the deep personal truth you may have never dared to expose, even to yourself. What would it mean to be *"you,"* (the "you" discovered above) every day? Pretend you're the director of your movie—because you *are*! Being director creates space between you and your life, so you can see and create without attachment to detail. Because your future hasn't been invented, you are free to write the story any way you like. As a movie director knows, *anything* can come next. You simply change the script, creating a story that evokes your greatest potential and dreams. This is not about planning or predicting a future, but about giving your dreams energy, "space" for them to manifest. The unconscious mind has no concept of past vs. future, or of reality vs. imagination. It hears only what gets repeatedly put into it.

Because it's an exercise, you can "play pretend." Your imagination is not limited by the same concerns that occupy your everyday mind. You don't need to include anything in your vision you don't want, anything you may see today as a problem. For the time being, there's no need to put finances, family obligations or other "stuff" into your vision. It is an exercise. You get to choose what you want in your life, and you get to dream big. There will be plenty of time later to solve problems of a new tomorrow, or to realize they've solved themselves!

Forget *how* things may come true; just imagine it all being so. Do this exercise regularly, each time changing and adding detail as you like (as director, you have this power), embedding it all in your imagination. Just keep loving your movie by giving your attention to it. Your movie *is* your love, so how hard can it be to love it? Remember, this isn't Hollywood: no need to sell 50 million copies; just one—to yourself. If you find yourself making this into a project plan, with dependencies and issues, stop; step back; restart. If you find yourself working with anything you don't truly love, pass it by; it is not "you." Why would you include problems if you're envisioning your ideal life?

IV: Action—*I Am*

> *"They say that time changes things, but you
> actually have to change them yourself."*
> – Andy Warhol

~~~ Act*: Take one step into your vision each day.* ~~~

Introduction: The fourth phase of the journey is, perhaps surprisingly, the first that calls for "doing something" in the traditional sense. In our action-obsessed world, the more contemplative stance of the first three phases leaves many saying, "I can't stand this; nothing's happening." If you've found that reflection, self-awareness and envisioning have opened you to a new perspective, then you'll find the action steps easy, especially compared to the "command-and-control" world you're leaving behind. That's because you'll now be drawing your energy from your awareness and vision, not from others or from willpower. Action is easy when fueled by clear thinking and inner meaning.

The Potential: I find it curious as I write this, but even this action step is based more on what I'd call "indirect action." You act by nurturing the conditions for your vision to manifest. You work on the context of your life, not the details. You allow life to unfold, rather than *make* it happen. With awareness, clarity and "memory of your future," you take one step, any step, toward your vision each day. What's different here, however, is that after each step, you don't just *keep stepping*; instead, you stop, look around, listen, reflect, absorb. Let go of how the step turns out and focus on *being* it. With each step, you're listening for *feedback*. Feedback is a natural information flow inherent in all living systems that tells the system how things are going. The answers you seek (how's it going, what to do next) are inside the experience of being it, not in a contrived, external measurement system or goal. One way you might view this step is that if envisioning creates a memory of the future, then taking action creates a memory of the present. Just notice.

The Obstacle: The greatest obstacle to taking action in this way is the influence of your old stories—about having goals, trying hard, controlling outcomes, measuring results. That's why the first three phases are so crucial. If you struggle here, resist "trying harder." Instead, go back and work on non-judgmental acceptance—of life and of your thinking, until you feel at peace with yourself and with life. By the way, voices in your head will still be telling you how scary it is to step into the unknown. The difference is that you don't listen. And of course, it's not "unknown." You've envisioned your way into it.

The Path Beyond: Your path in life is made by walking it, not by having planned it out ahead of time. Joseph Campbell, master of mythology and the archetypal human journey, said, "If the path before you is clear, you're probably on someone else's." Life is uncertain. No amount of goal setting, planning or predicting can make things certain. If you need proof, take a look at where life has brought you, right now. Could today be the perfect result of all your years of goals, planning and predicting? Most answer "no." The only part of life you *can* control is the way you see and think about life. The power of your own consciousness is more certain, and offers you more courage and comfort, than you'd hope to find anywhere in the outside world. It's time to listen to and honor your emerging inner truth. All the answers you need to fuel the life of your dreams are within the experience of being yourself, stepping into your vision, creating the path as you go. A vision lights your path from the inside; feedback lights it on the outside. No need to stop everything you're doing and create a new life. You can "take a step into it" each day, even if as an experiment. There's no need to plan an outcome, or even focus on there being one. Just be your truth, bringing your gifts to the world—in any way you choose. The sources of fuel to do this now include: (1) a growing freedom from the tyranny of outdated thinking, (2) a powerful vision that draws sustainable energy from deep inside you, and (3) a sense of meaning that the vision matters to you.

Example: Gandhi is always one of my favorite examples of living one's truth, of believing in self, of stepping into the unknown, of holding onto one's principle despite circumstances, of allowing one's gifts to unfold into the world, of listening to feedback … and by so doing, achieving results far beyond what any goal or agenda might ever offer. His life vision was that every human had the right to be treated with dignity. For him, to step into this vision knowing those he'd encounter didn't *care* about dignity (except perhaps, their own), and knowing he'd treat *them* with dignity no matter their behavior, took an amazing level of trust and commitment. The simple version of his life work is that he brought the British Empire to its knees with only a law degree, a loincloth, and huge commitment to a powerful vision of possibility. Change a few details, and this story could describe the Buddha, Jesus, Mother Teresa, Disney, M.L. King, and I suppose with a bit of modern-day stretch, Steve Jobs. You don't have to match their stories; to compare is yet another goals-based idea. Yet you have a dream inside you. Even better, you have all the tools to discover and manifest your unique dream. And it's a choice. I mean, it was a single choice, driven by awareness of a thought, that meant the difference between Gandhi changing the world and staying in the back of the train.

My Story: My big life shift, as noted earlier, from "getting things right" to "helping others get things right," was scary for me. I went from high-tech corporate "safety" (though I was no safer there than anywhere in the outside world) to creating a life coaching practice. I was on my own. This world was unknown. Perhaps it was tough to believe I had something to offer. Perhaps I'd not know what to do in strange situations. I was right. I *didn't* know what to do. But I did it anyway, one step at a time. And the feedback I got was that I *did* know what to do. I never knew ahead of time, but I knew "in time." This violated all my previous stories that I had to know upfront how it would turn out. How limiting. I built a coaching practice one client at a time. More accurately, I built it one conversation at a time. No, it was one *thought* at a time. Yet the potential and power have inspired me for 20 years now, and I feel "at home," at home in the unknown. In fact, only the external world is unknown. By being in touch with my authentic self, living my truth, I'm no more in unknown territory than I am in my own living room.

The Practice: Create what's possible now. In the previous phase, you created a movie of your future. By "showing up" in your movie each day, vividly imagining it, you create conditions for it to manifest. You can also envision individual pieces of life, at any time scale. As you stop several times each day to examine your thinking, notice whatever you were doing when you stopped (a project, dreaming about the week ahead, worrying what will happen next, fretting over how relationships will turn out, planning a vacation, wondering if you'll get the job you want, or how a tough conversation will go). Notice, too, where you encounter the edges of your comfort zone; your feelings will tell you. Now create a bold picture in your mind of exactly how things *could be right now* if you were living your authentic power to create the extraordinary. Trust that your inner self will know what to do here. Create a picture of things going extraordinarily well, a "mini-movie" *of this moment.* The more you *envision* "what's possible now," the more you *create* "what's possible now." With practice, you'll soon be able to envision the *next* moment while you are in *this* moment. This means that not only will you be able to see yourself being yourself, as it happens, but you'll also be able to choose *how you want to be* in the next moment, then *be* it.

This exercise might be seen as a warm-up for stepping into your vision. So, as you feel comfortable, take one conscious action in the direction of your authentic self each day. It matters far less what the step is than that it takes you toward your truth, and that it holds meaning for you. If you find it easier, treat this as an experiment; just try something out. Seeing it as an experiment frees you from any remaining concern about perceived consequences of stepping into the unknown.

Life is uncertain. Despite old lessons to avoid mistakes, to look good, to control how life goes, and to be concerned about what others think, we have little control over those things. What if, as part of your experiment, you could consciously hold those fears in abeyance for a day and try something you see as risky. If it's an experiment, it wouldn't even matter if it went wrong. The common question: "what if it doesn't work?" The important question: "what if it *does*?" Think of something you've both always wanted yet perhaps feared. Do it. Let go of the fight. You only *think* you control life. You control only how you *respond* to life. Experience what is and live the *process* of life. Labeling something as a game or as an experiment gives your mind the freedom to "try it anyway." Yet the *felt experience* of it is real, and herein lies its potential.

Whether you take this first step for real, for fun or with something trivial, it's important to let go of outcomes; focus on *being* your truth. Just focus each day on energizing your dream. Your daily actions create felt experience that undeniably leads you into your deepest truth. In *being your vision* purposefully each day: (1) you experience something new, consciously; (2) you realize you're still alive after stepping into the unknown; so you begin to build self-trust; (3) because it's only one step, your other foot is still anchored in the comfort of all you know; (4) the felt experience of being your truth gives you a taste of *feedback*. Instead of judging each step, feedback will let you know how things are going, and what to do next. No need for goals; your steps are created by walking them, and listening to feedback, not by having them laid out ahead of time. Just be yourself and be *with* yourself. The next step is easy: repeat the first step. Over time, you come to act from, and trust, your vision, not your old stories.

You soon realize, perhaps even as an *aha* moment that seemingly came out of nowhere (except it didn't), that you're living your dreams *and* feeling at home doing so. If you discover that the actions you're taking in living your truth exists as a "job," go for it. If not, you will have built such energy that you probably couldn't stop yourself from creating a job on your own ... or better, just doing it anyway because your love and your life are the same. It's been said that a life well-lived is one that finds "home" where your own passion meets the needs of the world. That idea even sounds peaceful.

V: REGENERATION—*I BECOME*

"When you make a world tolerable for yourself,
you make a world tolerable for others."
– Anaïs Nin

~~~ Sustain: *You become who you practice being.* ~~~

Introduction: So by now you may be well on your way to being your authentic self, every day. You certainly have the tools to do so. Yet despite the meaning your steps into your own truth may hold, despite the inspiration you may evoke from inside you each day, despite the personal freedom you may feel when involved in what you love, "staying the course" isn't always easy. Not every day will go well. You may not find a lot of company on this road; it is, after all, *your* road. There will be those inevitable setbacks. You may well doubt yourself. Others may try to talk you out of following a different drummer, even though the drummer is you! The last phase of this journey is to *sustain* the momentum, energy and trust that have brought you to this place so far. The work here is essentially to "coach yourself into becoming yourself," each day, as a way to continually *be* yourself regardless of life's challenges and circumstances. It's a way to ensure you're "always becoming," continually regenerating, refreshing and renewing yourself, from energy already inside you.

The Potential: Possibility is everywhere. *Your* possibility is all around you. Only your perception determines if you notice or not. Only your choice then determines if you take action or not. Both depend on conscious awareness. Few on this planet are 100% consciously aware 100% of the time. Yet through practice, you tip the balance of consciousness in your favor. Each step offers you just a bit more choice than in the moment before. Sustainability.

The Obstacle: Old assumptions, beliefs and lessons tend to stay lodged in the unconscious mind. Courtesy of its mission to protect you from what it thinks is danger, it continually ferries these old stories into your thinking and behaving. Only your level of awareness determines if you move beyond them or get trapped by their attempts to stop you. It's easy to slip back into unconscious living; the old voices in your head telling you to stay "safe" instead; the old voices of those you know looking for company in going along with the crowd; perhaps even your conscious voice telling you it's hard work to be yourself. The voices will always be there; what's different is that you now have the choice how you listen. The choice comes from awareness. Awareness comes from practice.

The Path Beyond: Regular *practice* keeps you awake, alive and aware. Here, you learn to become **self-referencing** (using self-trust and feedback as ways to assess your life's quality, not external ones such as opinions, judgments, goals), and **self-sustaining** (generating your own new perspectives and insights, and designing your own practices so as to incorporate new ideas into your everyday being). Self-confidence is natural when thought, emotion and action are aligned.

Sustain your vision and inner truth for a lifetime by adopting personal practices in three areas of life: (1) extreme self-care, (2) trusting your inner truth to guide your life, (3) connecting deeply—with yourself, nature, higher power, community of support. Practice allows you to "be with yourself," to *become* your vision. Working on your environment, or context, allows you to create a huge "stage" upon which your authentic life can unfold, powerfully and easily. **You** fill the space you've created— simply by stepping onto your stage, being your true self.

Example: If you look back at those in history we know as examples of living authentically (largely, we remember them simply because they *did* live authentically!), you find they sustained their journeys with practices such as the three suggested here. They were committed to exceptional self-care, learned to reference life from inside themselves, and had strong communities of love and support. Few of us live this life so well alone. We find support, both from inside ourselves and from the caring of others. Threads of a sustainable life are woven into a powerful fabric of support. You might think of the environment that sustains your journey as invisible basket, woven of the threads of meaning your authentic self has always been. The basket cradles you and your journey.

My Story: I'm so very much a student in this space, it's a huge piece of my work these days. I generally do well at self-reference. I believe in and trust myself; rarely do others ruin my day. I'm moderately effective at self-care, still finding myself drawn by old lessons to care for others over myself. I'm aware it doesn't always serve me, and I "know" that if I can't breathe, I can't help anyone else. I work on this every day. And as an introvert, a "quiet creative," and a product of Pilgrim/Puritan DNA, connecting deeply with others is not often easy for me. I cherish those with whom I do, and I cherish the communities of which I am a part. At the same time, it's all practice. The practices suggested below support me, too … in living authentically.

The Practice of Self-care. We are multi-dimensional beings: *mental, physical, emotional, relational, soulful, spiritual,* at the same time. Living fully means experiencing life in *all six* dimensions. Although the inner self wants balance among these, lessons from the external world tell us to rely more on the mental dimension (know/try/do). We pay a price for listening, however. The other dimensions thrive on quiet reflection, noticeably absent from our lives. Yet in those dimensions lives your unique, creative essence. Like a wheel missing spokes, you don't "roll" well if you honor only one or two dimensions. You find your sense of place in life—who you are and what matters most—by adopting a daily ritual of practice to honor all aspects of your humanness:

> *Mental:* the thinking mind, intellect, reason, cognitive understanding. Your mind wants creative stimulation, which can be found in reading, learning, writing, problem solving, managing life's affairs, envisioning a positive future, personal awareness and self-observation.

Emotional: the heart knows only love, and wants to give and receive love, which can be found in the pursuit of creativity, being in nature, giving to and receiving from others, and in connecting more deeply with the emotional reality of others with compassion.

Physical: the body wants to be vigorous and healthy; it's the vehicle for doing your work in the world. Your body is a source of great wisdom; it stores all of your memories in its cells. You open yourself to this wisdom by listening to it, and by taking good care of it, through exercise, nutrition, and offering a healthy environment for it to live in.

Relational: humans thrive on a sense of belonging, not only the connection with others, but also the energy of the collaborative—community. Healthy relationships are chosen, not given, and require nurture, whether with family, friends, clients, community or planet. Living with respect, reverence and compassion is to give *and* receive.

Soulful: soul represents the depth of your uniqueness, seat of your creative essence, life purpose. The soul wants to express this uniqueness as the driving force in your life, if only your head would stop saying "no". Because the soul speaks indirectly, you need create both space and ways of listening that allow you to make the connection.

Spiritual: spirit helps you feel a part of something far bigger than self, your connection to the divine, sacred, life's unity, a higher power. Spiritual connection is also subtle, rarely showing up in either the rational mind or in the midst of life's noise. The natural world is perhaps the best backdrop for opening and experiencing this connection.

Start with those that touch you in some way. If you can't imagine time for *any* of them, take some more time to get to know your thoughts. Release the ones that no longer serve you. Here's a list of more practices commonly associated with self-care. Adopt a new one each week or two and add it to your growing commitment to self.

Exercise: walking every day is ok for almost everyone; start simple

Eat healthfully: keep your body in shape so it can serve you in return

Quiet time in nature: renew and refresh your connection with all life

Listen to inspiring music: connects you with your deeper self

Watch a sunrise once a week: purposeful focus on new beginnings.

Have fresh flowers in your home: a reminder everything changes

Say "yes" to something new: expand your horizons

Say "no" to something that doesn't serve you: feel the power of "no"

Have fun: do something outrageously fun for yourself for less than $20

Simplify your life: minds are clear when desks and homes are

Adopt a culture of learning: curiosity is an amazing guide

Want less: consciously choosing to want/need less creates freedom

Look in the mirror: that's *you* in there; celebrate.

The Practice of Self-reference. Clarity acts as a "filter for the unnecessary." You no longer need to *think* so much about what's right for you; your authentic self handles it. In a few moments of quiet time each day, absorb the "you" you're becoming. Replay in your mind parts of your day or week, and notice yourself being you. Notice your choices and the impact they have on the results you experience. With time, you realize that the life you experience is the one you create, in each moment, with your thoughts, words and actions. Subtly, your "reference system" shifts from one based in opinions of others to one based in your own deepening sense of self-trust. Authenticity.

The Practice: Connection and Community. You are part of many communities. As is true in nature, communities are ecosystems—collections of pieces united by common purpose. Reflect quietly a few times a week on the communities of which you are a part. You might include self, family, friends, workplace, nature, faith, town, nation, planet. Notice how you contribute to each, and how each one contributes to you. Notice how, in their most positive sense, communities help expand the "you" you'd otherwise know, and how *you* expand the community to something bigger than it could be without you. What *meaning* do you find in how *your* life story overlaps the *community's* story?

AN INVITATION

Ordinary thinking will get you through an ordinary day. If you're content with that, you may find the idea of living authentically difficult or less inviting. But if you truly want to experience the extraordinary, then you need to tap levels of consciousness deeper and wiser than what you need just to get through an ordinary day. That takes courage, patience, persistence, and a strong support system. If you find these practices, especially the later ones, difficult to understand or to do, you might start by examining your patience and persistence with them. What you discover will tell you what you need to know—it's "feedback."

By adopting practices suggested here as everyday companions in your life, you'll be shifting your thinking to be far more inclusive and more aligned with your own personal truth. With felt experience of practice, your new thinking creates a true map to the territory of *your* life. You may even find, as I have, that the combination of conscious thought and a more inclusive context helps make decisions for you, thereby releasing you from the stress of life's little choices. What you will have done here is exchange the outdated, unconscious "cloud" of old assumptions and lessons for a filter created from your own truth—consciously chosen with deep clarity—as the context of your authentic self. The new filter renders most choices either so obvious you don't have to agonize over them, or so inconsequential they don't have to be made at all. The little stuff just no longer gets in the way of the big stuff.

Working directly with your thinking is one of many paths that lead you to your authentic self. That's what this chapter is all about. Two other paths are offered here as well: Chapter 4 works with your everyday communication—*Constructive Conversations* and Chapter 5 works with your connection with nature—*In Nature's Image*. As you work your way through the path offered here, you may find one or both of the others intriguing as well. Different experiences, different paths, same "destination"—living authentically, the unique "you."

Lastly, I've often found it helpful to have a "complete life model" as a guide, an "invented context" if you will, one that brings many practices and ideas together into a unique way of seeing and living your authentic self. Here's such a model—called *Life as a Game*. The basics of this model are courtesy of Dave Buck from Coachville. I've always loved the directness and simplicity it offers. Living authentically opens up a world of adventure, exploration, chaos and uncertainty. Life in this world is more like playing a game than it is like "work" as we know it. Try it on if you like. Make life fun!

Here's how you might consciously choose to view your life as a game:

- Choose a *game*, a game *you* want to play. It's your life, so who better to say how you want it to go? Unsure where to start? How about this game: *to be the very best at what matters most to you*. That's a cool game, because no one has the potential to be a better you than you.

- Define the *rules* of your game. It's your game, so you get to define the rules, right? Start by using your own personal principles as game rules. Still unsure? "*The Fifth Agreement,*" by don Miguel Ruiz, offers five very simple life rules that can get you going. Either way, it's a chance to create a life where "stress" is not part of the rule book!

- "Play" is what you do to master *recurring processes* of your game. Name them. If you're not sure of *your* game's recurring processes, you could start with these: (1) know what truly matters most to you in life, (2) say *no*—to what doesn't matter, (3) say *yes*—to what does matter, (4) listen—to what your world, game and self tell you about how it's going, (5) learn—incorporate what you hear (feedback) into your game, its game rules, and its recurring processes.

- You master your game's processes through *practice*, which help you "be your game rules." Life is practice.

You practice by choosing to take the field each day—doing what matters to you, doing your best, loving to learn, enjoying challenge—regardless of conditions in your external world, regardless of the win/loss record. It's not about being perfect, or about winning; it's about continuing to improve.

- Create a *game plan*—for how you can make the most out of who you are. If you're not sure, start with this whole outline as a game plan. By being willing to learn, you create your life by walking it. Life is a possibility to live *into*, not an expectation to live *up to*. You, and life, change continually. Your game changes to reflect this, too. Revise any aspect of your game based on what you learn by playing it. The suggestions offered in any of these steps will help get you started; your experience of living them will guide you in making revisions so the game becomes uniquely your own.

- Learn to see things "as they are." It's your natural feedback system; (The way things "should be" is a dead-end street.) *Feedback* plus your commitment leads you to your next step, then the next. It's about knowing and accepting your own truth, no matter what.

Have *fun* playing. You're going to win some and lose some. That's why you chose a game you **love**—because it's *your love that sustains you* when the losses don't. Life is what you *put into it*, not what you *get out of it*. By the way, you'll get a huge amount out of it.

Living Authentically

... in a World That Would Rather You Didn't

Part III

Conclusion

Chapter 7

Conclusion

An Invitation to Possibility

"Truly, stories are the dreams of the people. We must create new stories out of our highest vision, and encourage our children to dream new dreams and build their world upon them."

– Manitonquat, Wampanoag elder, in *Return to Creation*

You might view the three pathways presented in this book as different "lenses," or contextual frames, for discovering and becoming your own authentic truth. Whether it be through conversations, through alignment with nature's way, or through reflection on your consciousness, you arrive at the same place—deep knowing, connection and **trust** in the true "you" that lives underneath today's, or yesterday's, lessons, beliefs and assumptions ... and all the unconscious, habituated thinking they spawn. The lack of self-trust you may have experienced, possibly for years, is not a result of life (or others) being difficult, nor is it a result of your perceived lack of skill, but a product of your attachment to a life context that was never really your own. No wonder anxiety or stress may have been everyday companions.

Although it's difficult to explain ahead of time, by now you may have replaced an *intellectual* knowing with a deeper, *experiential* knowing instead. Despite what we've generally been taught about the primacy of intellectual or rational knowing, it is perhaps the *least* reliable of our many "ways of knowing." When you discover, then listen to, the quiet, yet persistent voice of your own inner truth—"*I trust, I know, I am*"—a voice that continually speaks through all of life's noise, your old ways fall away on their own, leaving you believing in *your* voice over all others, and aligning your life with its message. You step into each day with an easy sense of confidence and trust you may have never known, or imagined, as possible. As you expand the edges of your seeing and thinking, the edges of your world expand, too, to include what you used to believe was impossible. The "impossible" things don't change; your relationship to them changes. New ways of seeing and thinking change your world. A sense of freedom and peace becomes your companion; it comes from inside you. No longer need you seek the energy from the outside world to negotiate your days. Your authentic truth becomes your own life-long sustainable energy system. It lives forever inside you.

History is filled with icons of this spirit. Perhaps that's why we know them. Thoreau, Emerson and Muir come to mind from the west. Gandhi, Mother Teresa and the Dalai Lama from the east. Jesus, Moses, and the Buddha from ages past. One thing all of them had in common was a deep belief in their personal truth. Each took a stand for a societal cause *based* in that truth, and held a commitment to something bigger than themselves. On one hand, most "had" very little, whether in the way of status, money, possessions, education or luck. On the other hand, each "had it all," a trust in their own potential, and the power to manifest it out of the limitless possibility the universe offers. In short, they took full personal responsibility for how their lives went. You have the same greatness inside you.

Accepting full responsibility for how your life goes is an act of personal authenticity. It also means releasing the blame game, 100%. If you are responsible for how your life goes, then you can't blame others for its struggles and challenges. As a matter of fact, it's not, and never was, an issue of blame. Everything in life has consequences. Consequences are results, but without the judgment so common in our everyday world. As in nature, a storm or earthquake has consequences, ones we often judge as "bad." But to nature, they're just consequences, and the process of creative expression continues, either to re-create more of the same or create something entirely new, beyond the scope of what could have been envisioned beforehand.

No one else can "make you" be, do, say or feel anything; nor can *they* be responsible for how *you* respond. **You** are. Your feelings belong to you, as do your interpretation, listening, intention and personal presence. While it all may sound scary beforehand, it's curious how much freedom you feel once you accept yourself and reclaim your power. As always, practice creates the experience.

From a place of personal authenticity and self-trust, you realize you no longer need to have agendas, to control other people, to know outcomes ahead of time, to be backed into a corner by the bad behavior of others, or to censor your own presence. You just "show up," *being* your principles, and choosing your context, then allow the *natural feedback* life offers to show you the way—to the next step, and the next. You need only listen. Because you can't possibly know or anticipate every path life can take, leading from self-trust and honoring life's feedback offer all the freedom, and skill you need to chart a course into each new day.

Transformation is up to *you*. No one else in your life needs to change or help. True, you may still get cut off on the highway; your boss may still yell at you; your spouse may still get angry at old behaviors. What's different is *you*. When you *see* old things in new ways, you *respond* to old things in new ways. *Your* world will change when *you* change.

I offer a simple invitation here—don't adopt *my* rules for your life (I don't believe I've even offered any), or the *world's* rules, but *your own* rules. Only *you* know the choices that work for *you*. If you step into tomorrow using yesterday's thinking, you'll create tomorrows that look alarmingly like yesterday. Taking a stand for your greatest potential sets you apart from the crowd. You once had the illusion of safety in numbers. You'll soon learn that the greatest safety and certainty you'll ever have or need in an uncertain, chaotic world is your own inner truth.

A word about today. Chances are quite good you'll encounter a lot of small-minded people on the path to your truth. Many will be people you know today. Living authentically sets you apart from the crowd. Choosing to see and think in ways that diverge from the status quo represents a *threat* to that status quo; so you won't get a lot of help from others. The status quo often affects us in the same way the unconscious mind does; it "preserves itself." Perhaps that's why it's called status quo. You may even find that the more boldly you step into your deepest truth, the louder the voices of opposition become. If the "prevailing wisdom" were that "wise," however, those same naysayers would be leading happier, more fulfilling lives right now instead of ridiculing you for the courage you're displaying to live yours. Those who spend their lives putting others down are not the ones changing the world.

A word about tomorrow. Both experience and observation indicate that we put a lot of energy into thinking about the future. With our busy imaginations, we can plan, desire, fear, predict, avoid or dream a vast array of possible tomorrows. All these imaginings, whether they serve our greatest good or inhibit it, seem to start with the perspective that the future is a very distant time and place. This long-term-only view creates two needless obstacles, obstacles of which we're generally unaware.

First, we're very bad at long-term planning or predicting, especially when it comes to things that are inherently uncertain. Stop for a moment and look at your jobs, relationships, health, finances, dreams or even long-term happiness. Are things going now just as you'd planned or predicted years ago? It's kind of a problem, then, with ample evidence to the contrary, that we still believe we can control how it will all turn out— way out there.

Second, we seem to forget, or ignore, that to arrive at a future place and time, we must pass through today, and tomorrow, and the day after, etc. It's almost as if our planning would have us "dropped into" some future world. (Everything will be OK *when* ...). By thinking that way, even unconsciously, we forget that what happens today matters—and is the raw material for creating tomorrow. With this often-unconscious thought form, we also tend to use the current moment mainly to worry our way to the *next* moment. This serves to deny us altogether of the deep, meaningful experience and possibility *this* moment offers. If we keep doing this, moment after moment, we never arrive at a place we love, because we keep missing the experience of love (now), lost as we are in worry about what comes next (then). There is no future there.

The path to your future cannot be laid out ahead of time; you don't predict or plan it; you *create* it. You create it as you walk. The walking *is* your future; walking is what happens right now. Seeing life this way, the future becomes a set of "fully experienced present moments," strung together one after another. It's this experience that creates a life you love. An extraordinary life is not one with all the drama of a Hollywood movie, unless that's what you want. Rather, it's about your ability to experience the extraordinary, in each *ordinary* moment of life.

You create a thriving future by learning to see and think about the present in new ways. The practices suggested throughout this book all lead you to that place—full awareness and non-judgmental acceptance of the present moment. With this awareness, your thinking becomes marked by greater clarity, perspective and objectivity than the thinking you need to get through an ordinary day.

By calming your mind, simplifying your life, caring for yourself in exceptional ways, getting to know your thoughts, coming to discover your deepest truth, and envisioning an extraordinary future, you truly transform your consciousness ... from a consciousness of *circumstance* to a consciousness of *possibility*. This means that what comes next arises from your consciousness, not what's going on "out there." As you embody these ways of being, you'll find that life unfolds naturally and easily into the new framework, or context, you've created by your new ways of seeing and thinking. You will no doubt also discover the underlying order and truth that live just below the surface of all life, including your own. Once you experience this order, you feel empowered to boldly step into the unknown, fueled by your own personal authenticity. As most original cultures knew and practiced, you "observe a new world into existence," thereby rendering your old world obsolete. This happens with a shift in perspective. You shift your perspective through the practice of noticing it!

True, you may not know just where this formula will lead you. After all, you are inventing it as you go. Also true, you'll never 'arrive,' but hey, there was never any 'destination,' either. You become this new thinking by the practice of doing it; you practice your future into being. Despite what you can't control, there are a few things you can count on. You choose what matters to you. You observe and experience the present moment. You change course based on the feedback you get. You can do all of these things independent of the world "out there," including how others think. It's your life; there's not a lot to be gained by living someone else's life instead. As a perspective on how your practice may evolve, consider this "map" you may walk as you create the path to your authentic self.

As your practice deepens and becomes more natural to you, you may find your shifts in consciousness move along this path:

- **Silence**—experiencing silence opens a pathway to inner reflection.
- **Reflection**—through quiet reflection, you become aware of your own thinking.
- **Conscious Awareness**—with growing awareness, you gain clarity of perception and perspective.
- **Clarity**—from a place of clarity, your own deepest truth emerges—about yourself, your work, others, life and the world.
- **Personal Truth**—you can now honor your truth through thoughts you choose to think.
- **Self-Trust**—with clarity and truth, you can trust your thoughts to guide your choices.
- **Personal Freedom**—making choices from your essence, you experience life as your own.
- **Peace and Meaning**—conscious choices, driven by thoughts based in clarity and personal truth, express what matters most to you every day, connecting you with all life.

Here's a repeat of a part of the Introduction to this book. From the vantage point of your new experience of self, see how your perspective on these aligns with your felt experience.

While discoveries you'll make in your journey are uniquely your own, the framework for personal inquiry tends to follow common threads for everyone. By adopting the ideas and practices suggested here, you will:

- Become willing to let go of the past, including who you *believe* you are, in favor of who you *really* are, the potential you may *become*

- Come to *know* yourself deeply, truthfully. Only by finding what is genuinely your own (instead of someone else's) can you truly *live* it

- Come to *trust* life, yourself, and your inner truth. Answers to the mysteries of an authentic, meaningful life are found only inside you

- Discover your *truth*, what matters so much that you want to design your life around its fulfillment (essence, uniqueness, passion, soul)

- Accept that life's *context* changes throughout life because *you* do. Living is a *process of continual inquiry, reflection and change*

- Choose *personal authenticity* over social acceptance

- Define and declare a *life context*, a huge "framework of possibility" for your life that embodies your intention, thinking and true self

- Be a *contribution*: bring your truth and gifts to a *community* of your choice

- Experience life's inevitable challenges and obstacles as *teachers*

- *Create "sacred work"* through the expression of your unique essence. If that work exists as a "job," go for it; if it doesn't, create it

- Experience nature as a connection to your deepest self, your source (this doesn't mean you'll end up hugging trees)

- *Be and do your best* in each moment. This means *remembering* your truth and intention, in each moment

- Listen to the natural *feedback* life offers; make continual corrections—to intention, thoughts, truth, words, actions—based not on a fixed agenda, but on how life's experience touches you each moment

- Treat yourself, others and life with *reverence* and *respect*

Only *you* will know what works ... for you. Taking a stand for your deepest truth sets you apart from the crowd. Congratulations. With practice, you will have become the inventor of an extraordinary future—your own.

COLLECTED PRACTICES

Collected and summarized here are the most significant practices from this book—perhaps a "quick reference" for use after you gain deeper experience with them.

Personal silence: A regular practice of calming the mind is a pathway to your deepest truth and greatest potential. Sit quietly alone for 20 to 30 minutes each day. Relax your body; take a few deep breaths. Breathe purposefully; listen. Just be present; there's no right or wrong. Thoughts may continually arise, often in the form of inner voices (things to do, fears, etc.) View them as clouds; just watch as they pass by. Silence focuses your awareness on the present moment. That's the moment you tend to *miss* while worrying about the *next* moment instead.

Observe your thoughts: Only by interrupting the incessant flow of unconscious voices you *think* is thinking will you get to know your truth. As an *observer* of your thoughts, you gain a perspective on your consciousness you'd never get as a *participant* alone. *Stop* what you're doing three or four times a day. During a few moments of quiet reflection, replay in your mind thoughts you've had since the last replay, as if a movie with you as its audience. **Listen** to what they tell you. Resist judging or trying to change them. Just notice.

Understand your conversations: Replay several of your conversations each day. Include some that went well, some that didn't, some you had with yourself. Notice *now* the thinking you brought to the conversations *then*. Notice how every conversation goes just as intended, intention determined by often unconscious thoughts. Notice how you listened—to learn, or to confirm what you already knew. Notice judgments you made, where the event itself differs from the story you tell about it. Notice your emotions, then trace them back to the thoughts that evoked them.

Discover your personal truth: Reflect on your life's big picture. Rather than a linear view from childhood on, review *aspects* of your life. Ideas: education, family, transitions, hobbies, relationships, jobs. Overlap is OK. As a replay, look *inside each aspect*, one at a time, separate from others. Ask yourself: What did I wonder or imagine? Who was I always being? What was I always drawn to? What did I do whether I gained approval or not? Find places in your "always" stories that caused contention with others, but you did it anyway. After considering each aspect this way, find what's *common* in your lists. As you discover who you can't *not* be, you're guided to that piece of yourself that is so naturally you that you may have missed your unique essence, soul, or purpose. It may take weeks or more for a complete picture to emerge.

Envision your future as a movie: In addition to being the *audience* in your life story, you're also *director*. As a director knows, *anything* can come next. Change the script; create a story that evokes your potential. This isn't about planning or predicting a future, but *giving your dreams energy, so they have space to manifest.* Sit quietly. In your imagination, create your future as a movie, with you as star, living the life of your dreams, evoking the heart, soul and spirit of the "you" you've perhaps never exposed, even to yourself. Imagine it all, making a great living doing what you love most. Do this exercise regularly, adding details. Fall in love with your movie. You need sell only one copy, to yourself!

BE your truth: Take one action step toward your vision each day. Let go of outcomes; focus on ***being.*** Just do or be something that energizes your dream—every day. Instead of judging each step, just listen—for ***feedback.*** Your daily actions create felt experience that undeniably lead you to your deepest truth.

Self-care: Caring for yourself creates self-trust, evokes emotional intelligence and improves your connection with others. Create a daily ritual to honor and respect the many dimensions of your being. Like a wheel missing a few spokes, you don't "roll" well if you honor only one or two dimensions. If you need a start, try these: *Physical*: walk, yoga, eat well. *Mental*: read, create, quiet time. *Emotional*: be with loving people, journal, create fun. *Relational*: join communities of like-minded others, build support systems. *Soulful*: silent time in nature, watch a sunrise. *Spiritual*: time in nature, inspiring music, connect with a higher power.

Connection and community: Reflect quietly a few times a week on the communities to which you belong. You might include family, friends, workplace, nature, self, social, faith, town, nation, planet. Notice how you contribute to each, and how each contributes to you. What *meaning* do you find in how *your* life story overlaps the *community's* story?

The practice of self-reference: The more clarity you have about yourself and your vision, the more it acts as a "filter for the unnecessary." You no longer need to *think* so much about what's right for you; your authentic self handles it. In a few moments of quiet time each day, absorb the *you* you're becoming. Replay in your mind parts of your week and notice yourself being you. Notice your choices and the impact they have on the results you experience. Resist temptation to judge or change anything. With time, you realize that the life you experience is the one you create, in each moment, with your thoughts, words and actions. Subtly, your "reference system" shifts from one based in opinions of the outer world to one based in your own deepening sense of self-trust.

More Practices

And here are some additional practices that can offer new windows into deepening your consciousness. Each of us responds in different ways to new ways of seeing; some of these might just offer a big new insight.

Observe thought patterns: One way to notice your thoughts with more depth is to trace *recurring patterns* over a lifetime. Sit quietly. Reflect on your life story. Do this exercise *several* times over many days or weeks. Each replay fills in more experiences and feelings. Go back as far as you can. Notice places, people, events, feelings, and the relationships among them. Notice the *significance* you attach to some things and not to others, how you weave a ***story*** about life, different from the simple facts and events. Continue to explore, noticing judgments you make—about yourself, others, life. Notice relationships among your thoughts, actions, and results. Recurring patterns, more than the events comprising them, teach you about yourself and your choices. Ask yourself what common threads unite all you've observed.

Create a larger context: when we experience obstacles in life's path, we often cite the facts and details as the cause. Life's details, however, rarely cause problems or hold you back; the issue is how you *see* them. You change the way you see and think by reframing, drawing a bigger box around them so more of life is included than is excluded. The bigger your thinking framework, the more life just "unfolds" into the context you define; you no longer need to fight or manage details again. Many times a day, stop; step back in your mind. View the current situation from a greater distance or larger time perspective. With distance comes objectivity, so things get less personal. What appears as drama in this moment is far less significant when viewed against a lifetime, or a month or week. As you continue to observe, you'll find that your edges both soften and grow, and that you release the tight hold you have on life, thereby becoming more resilient in the midst of a chaotic world.

Observe your belief system: After some experience with observing patterns above, you can begin to examine the belief system that *underlies* your thinking. Courtesy of your unconscious mind, you've *become* your beliefs. This creates a limit to the possibility you experience, however. Observation allows you to see now-unconscious beliefs, thereby making them conscious. During your daily quiet time, stop and examine each thought closely. For example, you may think, "I want to love my work, but there's no way to make a living doing what I love." Then *stop*; ask what old belief may be lurking under the thought. You might discover you'd always been told life is hard, work is harder, fun comes only "after work." You may decide that this belief no longer has the power to control your choices. Doing this practice regularly opens you to discovery of a host of potentially life-constraining beliefs.

Observe your definition of truth: How do you know what you know? What constitutes *truth*? What *evidence* do you need for something to be true? For things you *know* as true, discover *how* you know. Don't stop questioning until you do. Once you know, ask yourself what other way of *knowing* might be possible if you were to see this same thing from a different perspective. What possibility might open that was either invisible or unavailable with previously unconscious ways of knowing? Becoming consciously aware of your knowing helps you reframe your life in more meaningful ways. This is not about telling you what is true, or what to think or believe. It's about you becoming keenly aware of what truth means to you, and how you arrived at it.

Feel the feelings: No matter how much emphasis you place on creating a positive tomorrow, feelings about the past will resurface. I include this topic so you may begin honoring your feelings constructively, as an act of self-care, and not, as is common, by becoming *consumed* by them or by *denying* them altogether. It's also a great exercise in self-awareness, key to all the practices here. You may do this exercise any time you notice a feeling creeping into your life in an uncomfortable way (guilt, shame, worry, anger, resentment, anxiety, dread, etc.).

Feelings take you back to the place where unresolved stuff of life has taken up residence in your body. When you have an uncomfortable feeling, stop ... then:

- *Notice* the feeling; don't hide from it; don't think; don't try to deny or change anything; just notice the feeling.

- Discover where in your *body* the feeling shows up. Name where.

- Ask (and listen for an answer) *when* you felt this same feeling last. Not the last time the same event occurred, but the last time the same *feeling* showed up in your body the same way.

- Ask what that feeling *reminds* you of (perhaps the first time, somewhere in the distant past, when that same feeling occurred) Note again that it didn't have to be a result of the same event at all.

- Go back to that time. Replay the events and feelings of that first time. Discover what was happening for you that may have cemented inside you the reason you hide from the feeling today. Let yourself *feel* this.

- Now, name the *thought* that holds this feeling together *in the present*. Most feelings such as these are manifestations of thoughts. For many of life's "uneasy" feelings, the thought that created them centers on some version of "I'm not good enough." You might then ask if you have evidence today that this thought is true ... today. Clue: It isn't.

Be in nature: You are part of nature. Nature renews and refreshes. She nurtures and embraces. Denying the experience of that deep, primordial connection is a cause of the personal and societal malaise, stress, depression, and loss of spirit we experience today. Break the habit. For an hour or so twice a week, be in nature. Don't "do" anything; just experience nature's gifts. You might find a special location, so as you return regularly, you get to know it personally. Being in nature doesn't mean sitting under a tree talking politics; nor taking a back road to the mall. It's purposeful, quiet, reflective time in the natural world. If you need something to "do", *listen* to nature's messages; she offers all you need to unravel life's mystery. Ponder the word *reverence*. Despite its simplicity, and despite its initial awkwardness if it's new to you, this practice reconnects you with soul, spirit, the unity of all life, your own deepest truth, your higher power, and the center of your existence.

Walk: Your body needs exercise; your mind needs cobweb clearing; your emotions need a break; relationships need to include one with yourself; your soul needs quiet time; your spirit needs connection to nature. Walking does *all* these. You can walk regardless of the weather or your age. Thirty minutes each day is a good start; that's two miles if you get into it; it's a mile if you just want to absorb. Do more if you like. This may be the most significant piece of self-care you can do. A few criteria: walk in silence, even if with a friend; honor the time as sacred and purposeful, resisting temptation to make things-to-do or grocery lists; actively notice sights and sounds of nature; tune out whatever humanity you must deal with.

Adopt a culture of learning: What if life were more about learning than about achieving? What if mistakes were about learning, not about failing? What if emotions were teachers? What if stress were a signal and not a problem? Each of us tends unconsciously to see life through a *prevailing question*. In your practices to date, you may have already discovered this. For many, the question is of the form, "what's wrong?" When we see this way, we become dissatisfied with life, *and* find things to fix. The world "becomes" a problem to be solved. If instead we *chose* a new question, perhaps "what can I *learn* here?" possibility would open instantly. When you *look* for possibility instead of problem, you *find* possibility instead of problem! As you notice your own prevailing question in any of life's situations, see if you can consciously choose a new one. As you do, you start to see your life as a learning opportunity, not a problem. A few possibility questions, companions on your path:

- What's the greatest potential this situation holds for me?

- How many "right" answers might I find in this situation?

- How might I respond to life from the perspective of my own truth?

- How does my life go when I listen to my intuition and heart, compared to how my life goes when I listen to the voices in my head?

- How does my life go when I adopt a culture of learning (what's possible) instead of a culture of blame (what's wrong)?

Observing the spaces between: Despite attempts to know the unknowable, predict the unpredictable, control the uncontrollable, and convert all chaos to order, you can truly neither know nor control what comes next. A way to accept life's inherent uncertainty is to notice your experience of *spaces between* the things of life, not just the things themselves. I've had clients respond saying, "*nothing* comes between; that's what "between" *means*." I invite deeper exploration. Three viewpoints on the space between—home to the potential the next moment holds.

- **Big spaces**—how have you responded to major life transitions—a new job, losing a relationship, between homes, between seasons. How did you *feel?* (fear, anxiety, relief, denial, acceptance, joy, anger). How did you *respond* to the empty space thus created? Did you rush to fill the void ... with a new job, relationship or home? Did you slow down so as to learn and grow, to accept the natural ebbs and flows of life?

- **Medium spaces**—several times a day, stop and notice how you moved *from* one activity *to* another, from a task to a phone call, from work to home, from one thought to another. Were you annoyed, relieved, etc.?

- **Small spaces**—in your quiet time each day, consider consciously your experience of the space between your breaths, even between thoughts. Might even the smallest spaces in your life be openings to new possibility or insight? Is this not, for example, the home of your intuition?

Stop wanting so much: The energy fueling your life is very likely the energy of *wanting*. Most of us were brought up to think *having* more is key to happiness. As you go through your day, stop now and then to notice your "wanting." Just notice; no need to fight it off. You'll soon begin to see how much you already have, the person you already are, and the energy you create just by being that person. *Noticing* is the beginning of letting go of wanting. I once heard it stated this way: We learn we need to *have* stuff in order to *do* stuff in order to *be* somebody (or be happy). It's the opposite. When we can *be* someone (or happy) then we can *do* just about anything, which lets us *have* all we want. Be someone, maybe who you really are!

~~~

The missing ingredient in living authentically is consciousness. It's just as simple (and as difficult) as that.

~~~

*"A seed hidden in the heart of an apple
is an orchard invisible."*

~~~

*"It ain't what you don't know that gets you into trouble.
It's what you know for sure that just ain't so."
– Mark Twain*

~~~

*"When we no longer know which way to
go, we have begun our real journey."
– Wendell Berry*

~~~

*You're at your greatest risk of failure when you
blindly rely on strategies that worked in the past.*

~~~

*"When you follow a set of tracks back to its maker,
you unravel the mystery of its life story."
– Tom Brown, animal tracker*

~~~

*"There's nothing in a caterpillar that tells
you it's going to be a butterfly."
– Buckminster Fuller*

~~~

*"The veil that clouds your eyes will be
lifted by the hands that wove it."
– Kahlil Gibran, <u>The Prophet</u>*

~~~

ABOUT THE AUTHOR

For 40 years, **Bradford Glass** has inspired courageous professionals, leaders and their teams to challenge conventional thinking and instead take a stand for living with authenticity and freedom.

As a manager, as an educator, and as a coach, Brad has become known for both clarity of thinking and broad perspective—about self, others, life, work and world. He evokes in his clients a bold sense of possibility, inspiring them to release "the way it is" and step confidently into "the way it could be."

His coaching, writing and speaking draw on nature's wisdom as a model for living with creativity, resilience and balance.

Brad has earned master's degrees in engineering and in environmental studies, as well as the Professional Certified Coach credential from the International Coach Federation. He served as adjunct professor at Antioch University's Graduate School, and as a board member of the Waldorf School of Cape Cod, the New England

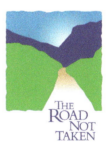

chapter of the International Coach Federation and Community Leadership Institute of Cape Cod. For 20 years, he led nature tours to some of North America's more unusual wilderness locations. In ancient times, he was a captain in the U. S. Air Force.

For a window into the journey to *your* potential, see Brad's website: *www.RoadNotTaken.com*. Brad lives on Cape Cod in Massachusetts.

CPSIA information can be obtained
at www.ICGtesting.com
Printed in the USA
BVHW020426031019
559866BV00006B/6/P

9 781733 254304